Love is a Hunt

Love is a Hunt

Written by

Jerr

Cover by

Bruno Solís de Campos

Dedicated to the invisible

Introduction

The reason I am writing this book is due to the amount of sexual chaos that is overwhelming our world. Men more than ever are alienated in sexual selection. The reason for this is that men are psychologically conditioned for submission to women which sets them up for exploitation. I write because I am a man and I believe in male power. I believe in my pride and I believe all men should live with dignity and respect. The world is going to hell because men are ignorant of the designs of women. These men are left to rot in digital fantasy while their female peers are lifted to power. The reader should be aware that I am not the man with the strongest frame or game. But I am the man who most cherishes the written word. My greatest skills are in rational thought, understanding behaviorism and my capacity for writing my thoughts. The man with the greatest frame is most likely illiterate and the man with the greatest game is most likely too consumed by pussy to have the energy or interest for books. It is not the man who has most perfected game and frame that will write about them but the man who most finds interest in reading and writing. It takes tremendous energy to read and write. And most men who are successful with women from a young age have neglected books. It does not mean that I do not desire women but rather my greatest love will always be for the written word.

Another key thing that weighed upon me while writing this book is keeping the message positive. I knew that I needed to be careful that I do not encourage promiscuity and irresponsible behaviors when discussing "Game" – Writing about game was a challenge but tempering my message to be responsible was doubly a challenge. It is each man's individual responsibility in his life and community to how he interprets and uses my message.

The greatest challenge a man will experience in sexual selection is rejection and neglect. I feel your pain my brothers. I feel your pain and have found a way out for you. The reason I felt the need to write this book was to give relief to suffering men. Once a man understands frame, he will understand the pain in his fellow man. And we must pick each other up in these twisted times. Do not give up on yourself. Realize that women are burdened by getting burned by greedy decisions. They get rejected not in sex but in the commitment after sex. Men must feel the pain of sexual rejection. An average man will get rejected by most women. And a man who is slightly above average will still battle frequent rejections. This a commonality among men. We must battle through the overwhelming rejections of our sexual desires. And I hope this book helps you in our quest in sexual selection. What is that quest? Each man must carry his own conscience. This is a book of power. And how that power is used will be different for each man. We have many men in our times that have never known a woman. These men should not give up hope but rather get wise. Get wise to the ways of women and how our polarity builds sexual attraction. Read this book and reread it. Keep getting stronger and apply the power dynamics into our life. And most importantly, stay proud my fellow orphans.

Animals

can

be

gamed

What does it mean to game something? It means to look upon the patterns of their behavior and alter hunting method for success. What kind of hunting? That depends on the animal. A man who is fishing will test the waters of various lakes to see which one holds more fish. It makes sense to fish in the watering hole that holds more resource. But once the man finds a good spot to fish, he will then test to see what methods work on certain fish. He will alter his lure and bait dependent on which has more success with the fish he is after. This requires patience and rational configurations of hunting method. A fisherman does not cry because a certain fish is refusing to bite his favorite bait. He coldly changes to what works. Hunting is about behaviorism and behaviorism requires emotional detachment. A hunter who gets emotional over hunting will make a bad hunter. He must become like the cold eyes of a tiger staring out from the brush. Looking and examining the prey before him. And he must apply humility in what works. That is the key. We test and we alter. We do what works and we abandon what fails. This is what it means to hunt.

In dating, why do we say that we "game" women? This language will upset feminized men because they are ruled by emotion and do not like the cold manipulation of that word. They do not like women being hunted because it reveals themselves as animals in behaviorism. See? It lowers the god in their mind to earth and makes them feel uneasy. They worship women and to game women is to worship weakness. This is the crux of female worship. It requires a man to mystify his mind over female behavior to strengthen the unknown power source. The more mysterious the power source the greater his trust can be in his authority. This is one reason that feminized men become emotional when confronted with the simplicity of female behavior. It takes a man who views himself as authority over women to coldly detach from their creatureliness. And women in realty are simpler and more creaturely than men. Men have been told lies to strengthen the female power source in their minds. It is supreme gaslighting that has groomed men for submission. The point of my writing from The Wall Speaks, Our World of Illusion and Shattering the Feminine Frame is to demystify women for men. Women are simple creatures with simple cravings. And there is a deep commonness to women that they hide by making men emotional. Emotions cloud rationality. And the more men are made to be emotional in their worldview the more blind they become to the weaknesses of women. In their minds they will then lift up women as noble and moral sages. This primes these men to respect women's authority while not respecting their own authority. Once a man shatters his emotional worldview, he will begin to see the light of rationality. He will become like the fisherman who alters his own behavior to best exploit the behaviors of fish. Women worship nature when they become less religious in masculine organized religions. A return to paganism. They worship THE GAME. But to worship nature is to worship the eternal battle between organisms. To worship nature in truth is to see that everything is in constant conflict. To worship nature is to worship animals eating animals. To worship nature is to worship death, decay and rebirth. But women would rather worship their Disney fantasy than reality. Men look upon nature and we summon method from madness. We become hunters only because we know if we do not, we will be hunted. This is the truth of all things. We are either manipulating or being manipulated. And this is what happens to men who are mystified by female nature. Instead of manipulating women, they become manipulated by women. Female power rises with male ignorance. And this is the power source that feminized men and women want to protect from the light of truth. They want to protect women from being demystified because they believe more in female power than male power. I do not. I believe in myself as a man and I believe in you because you are also a man. This is a book of male empowerment and we must empower our brothers from the exploitation of this feminist establishment.

How

an

animal

is

caught

Patterns. What repeats in behavior can be understood. True mystery incites fear and excitement because we cannot summon a method to contain the madness. If a man is paying attention, he will begin to see women act like women. They align themselves to the feminine consciousness from their innate collective mindset. This is because a woman biologically is a dependent creature both emotionally and physically on others. Her body floods with hormone flux that makes her rely on others for emotional regulation and makes her sensitive to group shame. This hyper sensitivity to group shame makes a woman conform to groupthink. A woman has shared biological meanings with other women and the body of a woman is rocket fuel to feminine conformity. This mass conformity is what heightens her common patterns with other women. Women make themselves common to ease their doubt from group separation. And this mindset is what allows men to easily see their behaviors for understanding. *Patterns.* By the time you are done reading this book, you will see the patterns all around you. And this will allow you to game women *because patterns can be gamed.* Women have shared motivations in romance from both biological imperatives and psychological conditioning from groupthink. Do women change from one generation to the next? Very little. This book will discuss the basic patterning of women that is true this generation as it will be true in five generations. It will discuss not just method but game theory itself. And once a man sees a woman as a gameable creature, he will then fear all female authority because he will see the futility in submitting to something that is easily controlled. Be brave my brothers and continue forward.

The

human

female

A woman carries eggs and a man carries sperm to fertilize these eggs. And a woman who becomes fertilized by a man will become pregnant. This state will expand out her body as she carries the man's genetic seed within her. Her body will stretch and deform as she becomes incapacitated with child. While she is incapacitated with child, she will need a protector/provider to secure her pregnancy. A woman's innate hormone flux and her innate understanding of child bearing will inform her decisioning in sexual selection. And for this reason, she will seek out MALE CERTITUDE to ease her female anxiety over her doubt of self, she will seek out MALE PROVISIONING and MALE PROTECTION to ease her child bearing fears. This is the human female based on her biological conditioning. This is how we have been surviving as a species since the beginning. But a woman will expand her sexual selection decisioning based not just on her biology but also on sexual competition with other women. A woman wants to be impregnated by the greatest seed. And what makes a man's seed the greatest? When he fulfils the biological imperatives listed previously and creates enough status around a woman to make other women jealous. Why do women innately want to make other women jealous in sexual selection? *Because their mass conformity creates deep passive aggressions that fuel their interactions.* To rise in status over other women is a form of escape from the clutches of the suffocating conformity which is based on individual female social cowardice. This cowardice fuels self-hatred in the group dynamic as women surrender to petty squabbles from the frustration at the restriction. They will peck at each other like chickens because they hate themselves from being weak to conformity. And so, they will create social drama at those who fall outside their group conformity while becoming jealous at those in the group who rise in status from the attention of a provisioning male who makes the other women jealous. A man who understands female jealousy will see that pattern repeated among them all. In a way, it is like a sleepy dog who is disinterested in a bone but who suddenly wakes up to defend it not because he desires it in truth but because another dog is going to enjoy it. This is why a man who can incite sexual competition among more than one woman will heighten their interests in him. It is not the "bone" itself which has value but rather the interest of others over the bone. This is value inflation. And this value inflation can only happen because women's innate greed over secured resource will trigger in them the will to fight over that resource. The more they are invested in fighting over the resource the more they become invested in the heightened value of the resource. This is why women will commonly go for men who already are in relationships. They want to fight each other in competition more than truly being interested in the man. It is not just about securing the man as it is about stealing the man from another woman. It is greed and this greed reveals patterns to be exploited. See? This book will explain the greed and how a man can trap and exploit the greed in a woman's heart for his own gain.

A

woman's

greed

A hunter figures out what lures the greed in his prey's heart. It is greed that most sexual decisions are made. Women base their sexuality on what is the best deal for them. And the greed of their hearts will lead them into this sexual selection. A woman will choose a man who stimulates her primitive biological need but also (in a non-thinking way) will fight over what her female peers' lust over. If a woman's sexual jealousy is triggered by another woman, then she will compete for that same element and that element can be different depending on the two women within competition. It is not the "Bone" itself but rather one woman's personal interest which sparks another woman's interest. And "The bone" has value not just from itself but because a competition has been started. If a man has a certain interest in a woman, he should become aware of a friend of hers that most incites her own innate competition. And then he will see what the "Bone" of their desires that they are fighting over. A woman wants to have the prized man of her social group. Not because she sincerely loves the prized man as much as having the prized man will incite sexual jealousy. Do you see? This is the key to unlocking what motivates women. A man provides a woman with what makes her friends jealous. Women love traveling not because they love to travel. They love traveling because they love talking about where they travelled for status and to make their friends jealous. This is the core motivation behind most female behaviors. *Sexual jealousy.* A woman wants to be the prized and special one in her mass conformed social hierocracy. This allows her the spotlight of supreme emotional validation while stealing the spotlight from her rivals. A dual motivation that lies in the heart of a woman. Spotlight on self and removal of spotlight on her sexual competitors.

In

the

beginning

What does it mean to frame a woman? It means to rise above her in certainty of self and belief in one's own authority. This is the core principle that I wrote about in The Wall Speaks. When a man is talking to a woman, what is the energy? Remember that opposites attract. And women are attracted to certainty of self because they hold great uncertainty over themselves. Their dependence on external validation from their ancestral sense of group dynamic based on their biological need has atrophied their sense of self. They use the group for emotional regulation and to reassure their sense of self. This causes them to easily fall into self-doubt, and why they seek a compliment in sexual attraction. Does a man get nervous talking to women? Then he is holding uncertainty over himself and doubts his own authority. This will repel women because they are seeking a confident and proud masculine leader. The starting point of learning how to game women is to summon the power to doubt them and to believe in the certainty of self over them. This can come off as "Arrogant and cocky" to people with low self-esteem or who misunderstand selection. But in truth it is a man's supreme confidence in self which pulls a woman into his orbit.

The confusing thing about this to feminized men is that the more confident a man acts with a woman the more anxious she will act.

And so, the feminized man will show more doubt to boost the confidence of his woman of interest because he has high emotional empathy (like a woman). This lifts the woman in confidence which makes her doubt the man's frame. A man who shows strength in his presentation of strength will stir the anxious self-doubt within a woman. And this is not a bad thing. Why? Because a woman always is in self-doubt. The woman who is confident over a weak man is not sexually attracted to him because she is in fear that she is over him. In her mind she will think "I am leading him... and who will lead me?" But when a man is confident in his presentation of self and the woman becomes more doubtful of her own presentation, she will think "He is certain of himself. Good. I am in need of a proud leader to help me" – See? Inspiring doubt in a woman is not cruel as much as it is following a woman's programming for seeking leadership. This is the problem with feminized men who think that becoming a woman's friend is the best way to her heart. What they do not realize is that they are boosting the confidence in the women they are interested in which makes these women doubt their leadership potential. When a man is on a date with a woman, he should be thinking "She is more nervous than me" – and this would be the truth. Women are nervous creatures looking for calm men. And a calm man makes a woman cling to him so that she may share that calmness of self. If a man is on a date, he should fake calmness as best he can and then watch as the woman begins to become anxious in her own self-doubt. The man will then see the sexual chemistry improve as the woman falls into qualification mode to him. Her self-doubt compels her in seeking approval. Why? Because this is her feminine conformity mindset. Women submit to strong frames because women are reassured by the strength of frames. And they mold themselves to fit the cast made by the frame. The more a man projects his certainty of self, the more the woman will alter herself to please him. She will doubt herself and believe him. A primordial dance between the sexes. *Masculine certainty that leads and feminine doubt that follows.* To inspire doubt in a woman is like inspiring a body into dance. We cast a shadow from our strong frame over women to incite them into qualification mode. A woman craves to be led because of her high emotional uncertainty. The calm and assured presence of frame is essential to inspiring this doubt. Do not think "She is better than me", instead just focus on your calm presentation regardless of the woman and then watch as she begins to doubt herself. This is the common patterns of all women and this is why a man will immediately see women fall into this behavior. Patterns.

Romance

A woman innately knows that her eggs are more precious than a man's seed. But a woman can be fooled. This requires a man to stop romanticizing women and to start romanticizing himself. A man must prize his seed over the woman's egg. When a man loves himself more than women is what draws their eyes. Why? Because women are used to viewing themselves as superior to men because most men are desperate for sexual access. This inflates women's egos as they become the choosers in sexual selection. Think about the female perspective in romance. An average woman will receive sexual attention from many men but the average man will be invisible to most women. The less a man gives attention to women the more he sets himself apart from the males that are sexually thirsty around him. What is the focus of his attention? His own masculine ambition. A man who can hold back his sexual thirst puzzles a woman and becomes a mystery to her. This is not to say that he is not sexually thirsty but rather that he is hiding that revelation from a woman he is interested in. A man must hide his sexual intent while giving subtle clues to his desire. This mindset fuels sexual passion in women. Think about what happens when a framed man is telling a joke. He does not laugh at this own joke which causes a tension in the air that pulls the laughter from others. If the man were to laugh midway through his joke would kill the tension necessary for inciting laughter in others. Same for sexuality. We build tension by holding back our own passion. Simps who compliment women's appearances and then cut straight to their sexual desires kill the erotic tension necessary in sexual selection. They lift up the egos of women with compliments of beauty which reveals themselves as desperate for sexual access like *the rest of the invisibles.* To romanticize self is to view a woman as privileged for association with that self. And this means to overlook a woman's specific ego values. Most women are overwhelmed by sexually thirsty men who inflate their egos. These men are quick to compliment beauty in the average woman because they themselves are disadvantaged to receiving sexual attention. When a man expects a woman to transcend her own beauty by directing the conversation to other aspects of her being makes her fall into qualification mode. By redirecting the conversation away from her looks makes her doubt her looks. And most women are egocentric toward their own beauty. To make them doubt their beauty requires them to figure out others ways to be of interest in sexual selection. Most women spend so much time in focusing their mind on their beauty that when they are forced to think outside it, they become anxious within that expectation. They immediately drop into doubt because their main ego focus is not being considered. *This is why a man should rarely if ever bring up a woman's looks in dating.* He should direct her to other matters and watch as she struggles in the deep end of the pool of her own thinking.

  A woman's frame of reality is innately weak which causes her to seek out men with a strong sense of self for her own ego association. Women share a man's frame of thought. This is why a man who loves himself will be loved by women. And a man who raises up women as more holy than his own self will be exploited/ignored by women. He doubts himself and this causes the women he is interested in to join that doubt. Women align their thoughts with each other and they share the mojo of the men they are interested in. This is why a man who romanticizes himself will be romanticized by women. He summons such a supreme self-love that projects that his seed holds more value than a woman's eggs. Women will fantasy about this "magical seed" because the man is not desperate to give it away like all the thirsty invisibles. The man who lifts up his pride over women will get their attention because of that very rarity. He inflates his own value by not giving away his pride to women. Weak men supplicate themselves to women. In their minds they think "I am nothing. She is everything. I am but a slave for her love" And this lowering of masculine pride allows a woman to wipe her feet on it before stepping over it for a man who protects his pride.

How can a man romanticize himself? He must inflate his ego. Women love confident men. And to be confident in self is to summon the ability to doubt others. Men who lack confidence are men who overly believe in the confidence of others. Pull away the confidence of others and place it on self. Look in the mirror. Look yourself square in the eye and say these words: "Many men have lived and died before me. And yet none compare. King Tutankhamun was laid in a golden mask and yet he does not compare. Thomas Edison lit up the world and yet he does not compare. Women are simple creatures with simple needs and they cannot compare. No single man can compare to my glory. The light around my face illuminates for others my glory. A thousand chariots from heaven come trumpeting my name. My death will trigger a thousand landslides and my final breath a thousand hurricanes. A golden mask would hide the glory. I am the one. I am the only. Through me others shall see God. A woman is privileged to knee before me"

Sound arrogant? Good. Summon the passion of self-belief. Fuel your own mojo. Women are mojo leaches. They want a man who has supreme self-belief that cannot be easily made to doubt. Think about that. A woman innately is ruled by self-doubt and relies on group approval for sense of self. A man must rise in belief over the group to lead them. See? This is why women love cocky/arrogant/confident men. *To believe in self more than others is to summon a leader's mind.* A weak man will doubt himself when doubted by the many. A strong man will make the many doubt-themselves by the certainty of his will. He validates himself which makes others validate themselves to him. A king's mind and seed made precious. Women love men who first love themselves. Women believe in men who first believe in themselves. And belief in self is one of the most challenging things a man can do. A man must rise from the thirsty invisibles and make himself known. He must transfer any self-doubt he may have and place it on the woman. She must doubt herself enough to believe in her man. This power transfer fuels erotic tension. Women crave leaders because women want to believe in a power source outside themselves. A singular power source that requires no energy from external validation. This is masculine frame. And this is game.

Before a man games a woman, he must game himself. Most men doubt their sense of self and this projects out to women. A woman's strongest intuition is in sensing out a man's own **sense of self.** Men who have strong sense of self are heavy anchors that draw women into their orbit. We are bodily vehicles that go from cradle to grave. And pretty soon I and you will be dead. Sound awesome? Of course not. That is why we must summon *power beyond belief* for ourselves. We must become excited about our own journey. And how do we do this? We see ourselves on a hero's journey. We conjure irrational belief that we are not just human but beyond human. When my heart broke, what was I thinking? That I was a pathetic nothing that got emasculated. And from that despair, I summoned a new narrative for myself. Instead of being a loser who got cheated on, I would become something more. I would become more than human. I would seize my body like a chariot under the hand of an ancient being. My spirit that controls me is not just "Jerr" – I am ancient of days. A thousand years is nothing to me. I have come to alter the scales between masculine and feminine consciousness. My finger will lower the feminine consciousness while my other hand will lift the chins of the fatherless. This power source within me is surging. Sometimes my eyes glow in fire. Do you see what is happening? MY SELF IS WHATEVER I WANT IT TO BE. And why not make it grand as hell? Do you hate yourself? Then burn that self-down and conjure a new self. Completely alter your own story and rewrite it with you as the central hero. Let your sense of self burn bright within you. One reason I am able to transcend bad times is that I can change my own narrative within bad times. A man can die a thousand times in his life and be born again into whatever image he creates. If a man is thinking "I am a loser" – then he must create a winner. Be the hero we all need. Be the hero you need. Be the hero that women sexually crave. The only reason that I continue in life is that I believe myself to be a hero and I believe the world is in need of a hero. This is exactly what is means to romanticize the self. Too many men are overly inundated with brain numbing entertainment with gluttonous slop that makes them hate themselves. They impotently watch as cartoon heroes kill thousands of faceless aliens. And while they digitally castrate themselves their women handle real world responsibility. These men must awaken to the real power inside themselves and seek responsibility for all things. View yourself as crucial to the world. View yourself as crucial to the great master plan of existence. Play a key role and do not take a back seat. Love yourself more than any woman could possibly love you. Create a new narrative within you and let the hero's image form and expand. Ride to glory on the hero's journey. And this journey has stumbles and setbacks. It is every day and will be this way until death. Become a golden god of your own making. Summon the power of self-belief and watch other's sense of self quiver in doubt before you. Women will see something powerful in your spirit only because you first summoned that power first.

One

life

We get one life. We get one chance to get it right. One breath from beginning to end. And a man starts at the bottom of sexual selection. There is much to work on to become sexually valuable to women. This can make a man feel overwhelmed by our sexual burden. Sexual competition can feel overwhelming to men. The long road up the mountain of our sexual selection can make us despair. It is this despair and anxiety that makes most men opt out of sexual competition and freezes them into a spirit of surrender. And this fear of competition is a fear of living. A heavy fear like weights on the chest. It is like having to play basketball against Jordan. When competition feels crushingly difficult it can make the game itself feel unfun. This state of mind can make a man opt out and fall into "Monk mode" A heavy burden that makes us feel frozen. "NOTHING IS FAIR" a man may feel about reality. And what does he do? He gives up on trying and falls into a defeated mind. But do we surrender to tough competition as men? No. We summon self-belief in order to make attempts while harnessing the discipline needed to improve our attempts. Stop looking at the mountain's peak and move the focus to a few steps ahead. While writing this I have been training myself to sleep with my mouth closed. I have been sleeping with my mouth open at night because of a deviated septum. And when I close my mouth, my oxygen drops and a feeling of panic spreads out over my body which causes me to gulp down air with my mouth. But I believe in my own power. And so, what do I do? I close my mouth and breathe the small quantity of air through my nose. A feeling of panic comes. But here is where mental power comes into it. I tell myself that I will not die and that the air is enough. And the panic leaves me which allows me to grow comfortable with the smaller portion of air. This training allows me to have **IMPROVED SLEEP** and during the night my mouth remains closed. But the feeling that I got when I would close my mouth before bed in the beginning made me think deeply about panic and how that effects our behavior. A short-term panic causes us to surrender to weakness. And surrender to weakness robs us of improvement. Think about a man who fears swimming in deep water. He is dropped into the water and what happens? His mind leaves him and falls into hysterics. This fear makes him lose rational control over his body which causes him to flail in wasted energy before sinking. Many people die from drowning not because they do not know how to swim but rather because they panic in the water. It is the panic that makes us malfunction into failure. What does it mean to be cool? It means to have low reaction to the fear of existence. And this coolness allows us to conquer existence. Women love men who are cool and in control themselves because women need rational leaders who do not sink from hysteria. And the great burden of sexual competition can make many men become hysterical and begin to psychologically flail about when they must swim in romance. These men get nervous thinking about having to lead a woman in calmness on a date. And when they get to a date, they become frazzled easily which makes them panic. This panic of control accelerates the fear and make them sink. How many men lose their nerves before women? Too many. It is because they know the steep expectations of good chemistry which makes them lose themselves from anxiety. Do not fear the waters. Do not fear. It is fear that is most damaging to our existence. Fear kills romance. And fear kills the body before it can be born. Think about life. Soon you will be dead. Dead as a doorknob. And you will be forgotten. If a man is a great father to his son, maybe he will be remembered as a grandpa. But most of us forget our great grandpas even if they were excellent. Do you see? No matter how hard we try we will be forgotten. And then our life will be done. Think about God throwing us into the water of existence for us to only flail about like mad in a panic before being removed from life by Him "That is it. You are done. That was your life" How sad that would truly be. We had one chance and we lost our one opportunity from nerves. This is life. We are at the party, lets enjoy ourselves. In the previous chapter, I talked about how a man should create a narrative for himself in a hero's journey. And to take that further, we must be calm among the chaos. It is a calm and cool attitude that will help us succeed in our endeavors. Most women view older men as more attractive than younger men because the older men are more established. But this is not just established in a material sense as much it is established in sense of self. Older men have learned to swim instead of sink. They have learned to calm their nerves into submission and use them like whips under the chariots of discipline. How can a man lead a woman if he cannot lead himself? See this is the key thing a man must remember as he approaching women. When a man brings anxiety to a woman, he incites her own innate fear of existence. It is as if he is splashing in the water by her and threatens to drown her in his own panic.

We are all placed at the bottom of the mountain in sexual selection and some of us who lacked fathers are placed even further down. This can make a man lose himself into a fear living. But listen closely, it is never too late to start trying. Have trouble with money? Get serious. I do not care if you are sixty years old. Have trouble making male friends? Get serious about it. It is never too late. Look at it like a challenge of improvement. Lift yourself beyond the burden. This is what all women want in a man. A man who is above the burden of life. And this requires a man to master his nerves. He must think rationally. "I am alive. A MIRACLE. I have a few years left. I BETTER HUSTLE. There is a lot I need to do but I am alive to do it. I will not surrender to fear and doubt. I will believe in myself and work towards success" – And this man will have success. Why? Because he has changed his mind which is the precursor to changing his body and environment. In my own life, it was not until I was in my thirties that I began to understand masculine frame and female nature. Think about how much time I lost to ignorance. This could have made me feel deep anxiety for not just losing time but also having to change my identity so far into my own life. But I knew that if I never changed then I would be only wasting more life. And life is meant to be lived. A man can make fundamental changes in a year or two. He can alter his identity, his body and his environment in a few years. Separate from the anxiety and begin to move the body forward. Be proud of your life and be proud that you were given an opportunity to live it.

Calmness

attracts

The reason I have gone into depth the pass couple chapters on calmness is that calmness is needed in approach. Just like in hunting, nerves scare the game and nerves can ruin the aim for the shot. We live in a time where men have been feminized. And what does feminization mean to man's sense of self? It means he will be in psychological imitation to a woman's innate biological state of uncertainty. When a man masters his nerves is anti-feminine and projects trust of his authority. And this projection of trust allows a woman to align herself with the calm frame of presentation. A woman wants to conform herself to a strong frame. When a man projects doubt in his sense of self, he does not allow a woman to feel comfortable in in that conformity. Think about a man with a dog. If a man is nervous, the dog becomes nervous. If the man becomes fearful, the dog will become fearful. A dog carries his owner's energy just as a woman carries a man's energy. And when a man is nervous this will spike the woman's nerves. Men who carry nervous energy repel women because the women will absorb the anxiety which overwhelms them. When a man becomes certain in his sense of self and frees himself of the feminine frame of moralizing doubt; he projects a calm frame for the woman to enter like game into a cage. This is why women will reject nervous men and will leave men when they are having a life crisis. The men's mojo becomes anxious and fearful which pushes the women away. A lost job is bad but the reaction to a lost job can be just a bad. It is the reaction of stress that has the strongest effect and not the just the stress event. Think. What makes a good leader? It is a man who has master of his sense of reality to not surrender when his surrounding becomes chaos. Like a ship captain in a storm. This is why a woman will reject men who show nerves when they are approaching or who show nerves on a date. How can a man lead a woman in life if he cannot even lead a date? This is why it is crucial for a man to master his nerves by building his internal fortitude with masculine frame. My book The Wall Speaks is a guide on building that fortitude and shows how to strengthen a sense of self. Both key aspects in lowering nerves for approach. But just focusing the mind on fulfilling the role can be enough for a man. Just like a firefighter, soldier or police officer; a man can become brave because it is the expectation of his role in that moment. A man who thinks "I am the leader. I am not going to show doubt or fear while interacting with this woman" will be a man who is playacting within the role that is expected of him. This will allow him to disconnect from his body of doubt and his emotional reality. His mind rises above himself in order to fulfil a role. And that raised consciousness will help him detach from the chaos inside. Women by nature our doubt filled creatures and a man merely has to act the role of brave leader in the initial interaction for women to see the dynamic they can submit into. When a man shows his nerves, a woman becomes emboldened in her calm authority. But when a man shows a calm energy, this allows a woman to stumble in her own qualification from doubt which further emboldens the man in his leadership above her. To see someone else become anxious is rocket fuel for bravery of self. And this can happen within minutes of an interaction with a woman. The calmer the man shows himself to be the more anxious the woman will become which increases his confidence over her. This is "Fake it until you make it" and is great practice for a man when he is making approaches with women. He will become desensitized to talking to women and will see that women share a common submissive anxiety around strong frame. Their anxiety is not a negative as it allows them to fall into qualification mode which fuels their sexual arousal. The core sexuality within a woman is submission to a proud and confident penetrator. When a woman becomes uncertain about her own authority of self around a man, she will join his frame to steady her sense of being. See? This is the sexual polarity of our species. And the key to the pussy kingdom. Male confidence and female doubt. Male doubt breeds female confidence which sours sexual chemistry. No woman wants a doubt filled and anxious penetrator. Why would a woman want to be impregnated with doubt filled seed? Feminized men who doubt themselves and who are indecisive are like trappers who shake the cage they are wanting the game to enter. Frame is a cage of attraction. The hunter must be calm before the prey.

A

woman

craves

fun

A woman wants to feel uncomfortable in a situation with a comfortable man. Remember a woman tunes her own feelings of safety based not on the environment but on the man's sense of calm in the environment. This is the same for dogs and children. They exist under the frame of authority of their leader and if their leader remains calm then they too will join that frame of thought. To build arousal in a woman is to place her in uncomfortable situations while showing her that you are comfortable leading her through the chaos. See? A woman is chaos and requires a leader to guide her from her own chaotic feminine frame. When a man can summon a brave face while remaining rationally calm is what reassures a woman during a stress event. Dating for a woman is a job interview for a leader. But that is not the thought a man should have. A date is a job interview for a follower under the leadership of masculine frame. See? The man is showcasing his leadership skills and sees if the woman is following along with respect and submission. This is sexual chemistry. Male leadership and female submission to that leadership. A man who is wanting to date women must understand this fundamental sexual requirement in our sexual selection. He LEADS the approach. He LEADS the conversation. He LEADS the woman through the experience of the date. Lead, lead, lead. Women's sexuality is based on being a follower and that is why they become highly aroused when they submit themselves to a framed man. And for a man to be a leader he must plan and implement that plan. He approaches a woman and leads her in a short conversation that intrigues her. His frame is calm which calms her. She may fall into qualification mode from being nervous about the approach before joining the man in his calmness. This is brief roleplay for future possibilities which will spike the woman's interest in the man. A leader does not ask with doubt, he commands in a smooth way. "Here put your number in my phone" – This is both nice and bossy. See? And then he allows the woman to ponder over him for a short period of time. Remember, a woman must create the fantasy herself. Her imagination is her best friend and a man's mystery is what incites the imagination. And a man should only communicate with the woman with purpose. Note that. PURPOSE. He should communicate to set up a date. Many men will act like women and will reveal their intent by texting "I like you" – or simp behavior of "I think you are hot" – Or they will message the woman with something as mundane as "How are you doing?" – Remember, talk is for women. We must showcase through action. Action, action, action. Intrigue the woman in approach with social ease while demonstrating skills in leading a conversation. Get the number and then allow the woman to fantasize for a period of time. Then communicate to set up a meet up. Wanting to chat like a woman with a woman before meeting up on date is anti-seductive. See? Good chemistry is business like and it is direct. Both leadership qualities. The more a man understands that romance is about masculine authority demonstrated by his example, the more he will improve his skills with women. A woman is going on a date with a man because she is looking for a leader to calm her innate emotional anxiety.

Men should set up dates with women in active environments where conversation is secondary to the experience. Think. Women get together with each other to talk. They will sit and talk, talk, talk. The more a man talks to a woman on a date the more she will view him as a woman which will friendzone him. If they are chatting among action settings is what builds mystery and excitement. I will not give mindless examples of action dates because each town is different for each man. But the key is to plan something involving movement and a small amount of fear for the woman. The woman becomes anxious and the man's calm leadership subdues her into his frame. She becomes both sexually stimulated while being calmed under the man's authority. A woman is a duel being by nature and her sexual arousals has dual components. She wants to be afraid then reassured. She wants to have anxiety then be calmed. See? *Stimulate then pacify.* Raise then lower. Up then down. A woman's prizes her emotions from positive to negative. Being in love is like being on an emotional rollercoaster. Boring men reassure, reassure, reassure without inciting fear or doubt. Boring men pacify without first giving stimulation. Boring men do not know how to play with emotions which causes women to abandon them for "Fun guys". A typical fantasy for a woman is to be attracted to a man on a motorcycle. This is from multiple reasons. It is more risk taking then a man who is driving a car. It is more adventurous. But it also allows the woman to sit in the rear of the bike (Follower position) with her hands wrapped around the man while being stimulated from a fear of loss of control (Key to female orgasm) and reassured by the man's ability to lead her through the risk/adventure/anxiety with calm certitude. See? This is the fundamental principle of sexual desire and how to excite a woman during the early stages of dating. Exciting environment with calm leadership. Many times, in my writing I have compared framed leadership to a captain on a ship. And a captain's role is solidified in storms and chaos. A captain is made known by storms. That is when the captain earns the respect of the crew. He becomes the eye of the storm and does not let the chaos effect his frame. *Chaos effect his frame.* This is why action dates are better than "talk" dates or heaven forbid movie watching dates which have neither conversation or action (Unless a man wants to make out with woman in back of mostly empty theater which has a thrill to public indecency that women find fun) A man who invites a woman into an environment that makes her uncomfortable while he reassures her with calmness is like catnip to women. Many men fail in romance because they fail in understanding leadership. Leadership is the root of romance. And a man can learn more about romance by reading books on leadership skills than he can from most books on game. And it is leadership that transcends what most men are taught about romance. Men are taught feminine frame ways to supplicate to women. They are taught to raise up women as precious and holy things which causes them to doubt their own authority. A man who is taught to treat a woman like a queen will increase his own anxiety when the time comes to lead her. And a man who treats a woman like a queen will inflate her ego which will end up deflating sexual chemistry because she will begin to view herself as too good for him. Women only want men who they view as "Better" then themselves. They want a proud and powerful masculine leader who can guide them from their own bodily chaos and who has mastery over what they fear. A brave leader who can hold their hand through stressful moments. This is all foreplay to sex. This is what women crave in a man. Women give clues to their arousal but then hide them behind feminine frame of authority. For example, a woman will say "I want a decisive, confident and direct man" But she will not say "I want a leader" See? That is feminine desire hidden from clear view. And why would a woman confuse men by not being clear about her ultimate desire of craving to be in submission to masculine leadership? Because most men are weak which makes women fear submission to them. And so, they give small clues. A man should not become angry at women for what they are. Women submit to framed men for the betterment of our species. If women just submitted to weak men, our species would have died out long ago.

We

detach

from

emotion

The more emotional a hunter becomes about the game he hunts the less effective he is in the pursuit of the game. And this is the same with men in dating. To game a woman is to be emotionally detached from the experience. Why? Let us break down what sexual rejection does to our emotions. A man will have his hopes on one woman and he will pursue her only to be rejected which dashes his hopes. This will sour his emotions. If the man had high emotional investment in the woman he will become emotionally frazzled by the lost. This occurs when a man begins to fantasize about an infatuation he has been eyeing. His mind will center on her and when it falls apart so does the man himself. He falls apart because he invested too much of his own ego in association with the woman and when she rejects him; his own sense of identity falls in doubt. This increase in doubt over himself will further hurt his chances with other women. Why? Because women all seek a man with a strong sense of self. The main reason a man should be cold and emotionally detached in the early stages of sexual selection is that women are fickle and flaky creatures. Their reasons for sexually rejecting a man in the early stages of dating is high and varied. They protect their eggs from perceived weak seed and they are highly sensitive to whatever triggers that warning. They are easy to reject a man in the early stages if he is perceived as weak or at least weaker than the next man who is giving her interest. Think about women as birds in this instance. There are all kinds of reasons birds get spooked when being hunted. If a man has his sights on one bird and it gets spooked for any reason; he does not quit the hunt. He reevaluates his method of approach and tries again on another. Let us break down rejection on both sexes. *A woman sexually rejects most approaches by most men.* Women are the choosers of our sexual selection. Successful game requires high number of attempts while accepting high amount of rejection. A woman does not get this high amount of sexual rejection in sexual selection. If a woman wants to have sex with a man it is relatively easy for her. But a man must accept that he will be rejected by most women. Even men who are good at game still get rejected frequently. This is the key reason that a man should look at game from a high rational perspective and not an emotional perspective. He should look at it as a numbers game. Approach ten women. How many rejected the approach? How was the energy? When a man is first learning game maybe all ten women will reject him. This desensitizes him from the anxiety of rejection which increases the sexual chemistry for his next approaches. Maybe out of his next ten women he approaches, one or two women will show interest. See? As men we must accept that sexual selection is mostly a losing game with few exceptions. Keep track of the approach methods. Thank coldly about the failures and successes. Then alter the next method when approaching. Many men will become disheartened by sexual rejection which is normal since rejection hurts. But that is merely a perceptional issue. Rejection is coded into the game itself. Very few men on earth can approach ten women and get sexual interest from all ten women. Even men who are good at game will have numbers like three out of ten successes. Those are considered good numbers. This is why a man should realize that birds have many reasons for getting spooked when hunting them. They fly away from all kinds of distractions and noises. We learn how to best get close to them for the kill by altering our own behavior and methods. Remember women are skittish and flakey in sexual selection because they sit on eggs like birds. They do not want to be burdened by weak seed and so they scan a man of any personal failing. They scan a man of any doubt of his self and life. They listen to a man for any childish verbal vomit spit out over weak nerves. We must detach from the pain of rejection because rejection is the game. Rejection hurts women more so because women will say "No. No. No" to most men and invest themselves in a few of interest. They will emotionally invest themselves in days, weeks, months of fantasy. And then when the guy rejects them, he is rejecting all those wasted moments. Also, the woman will take it personally because sexual rejection is rarer to women which makes them sensitive to its effect. Rejection is common to men. And it is not just common to losers; it is common to ALL MEN. Take heart that you are not alone with this pain. It is part of being a man. We see a beautiful woman, we approach, we take our shot and we get knocked down. What do we do? We dust ourselves off and try again. The good thing about being a man in sexual selection is that we see women by in large as more attractive than women see men. When we get sexually rejected by an attractive woman, we may feel a loss. But then another attractive woman will walk by in a short time which again strikes our attention. Men have very little power in the beginning stages of romance. We only get power after a woman emotionally invests herself into us after the initial stages of dating. And once the power flips, we have the power to reject the woman who invested herself into us by denying her a relationship.

Emotionally detach. Do not think "I have been eyeing this beautiful woman for months and I am going to take my shot" No. Rather say "I have been eyeing these ten beautiful women over the course of a few months and I will take my shot with all ten. Then I will see if one of the ten is a success" This is anti-feminine. This is cold. This is the masculine way. We have an uphill battle in sexual selection and the sooner we enjoy the suffering; the sooner we can detach our identity from the suffering so that we can best alter ourselves to overcoming it. But do not let a woman know of this strategy. Why? Because while women do not feel guilt in rejecting many men, they do not realize this causes men to make attempts at many women. Women are emotional creatures and they do not like when sex is depersonalized. But they have created a brutal and depersonalized game for men to play. If a woman was transported into a man's body and had to play the game she created, she would fail and become disheartened. Why? Because she would not be prepared for the high level of rejection that is built into the game of her own design. She would approach like a woman; she would eye a fellow woman for a long time and then take her shot only to fail. Then she would crumble from the rejection. She would say "I had all my hopes in this one woman and she dismissed me just like that?" But unlike men, a woman will think about quitting. She will think "This game is stupid. I am going to retreat" Whereas a man will think "This game is hard. How can I alter my behaviors to best master this game?" The more experience a man gets with women the more commonalties he will see among them. And he will begin to understand his own behavioral failures with them. A man will think "I came off too needy and scared her away" Or a man will say "I failed in leading the conversation and this killed the chemistry" Or a man will say "I was too nervous and that made her nervous" - See? We do not say "Women do not like the special person in my heart. Women are cruel creatures and life is too hard. I am going into monk mode" This is why "Just be yourself" is damaging to a man in sexual selection. Because to be rejected for self is hurtful to self. But this is why we detach from the sexual selection process. We do not think a woman is rejecting us in truth but rather rejecting our methods. Same for hunting. If a hunter scares the birds away, he is not thinking "I am not made for bird hunting" No he alters himself to be a better hunter. We do not surrender to "Just be yourself", we OVERCOME OURSELVES. Sexual selection for men is a brutal game with constant rejection. It is not for the weak or sensitive. The game itself can only be played by men because it requires low emotion and low ego in configuration for success. Note that. Low emotion and low ego in configuration. If I fail in romance, I do not think "This woman hates me" but rather "This woman did not like my method" See? We blame the methods; we do not blame the self. This is what it means to hunt and this is what it means to game women in our sexual selection. All women are practice in sexual selection, even the ones we love and if a practice woman turns into something more than good.

Greed

can

be

gamed

How do we trap an animal? We appeal to its base greed. We lay out bait for entrapment. And what is a woman's base greed? Positive social attention that makes other women jealous. This is the key to understanding women's motivations. Do women love powerful men or do women want to be seen with powerful men? There is a root meaning to a woman's base attractions but the core element is that a woman wants to be seen. Would a woman want to travel to a beautiful destination if she could not speak of it to others, and she was not allowed to take pictures of herself to show to others? This would sour the whole experience for her because it steals what she most craves. A woman will plan a trip in order to showcase that trip to her peers. It is the showcase that gives women supreme pleasure. This is what a man should be thinking when he is discerning his own presentation of self for sexual selection. Women love muscled men because of a root motive of wanting a strong protector but the greater reason is that a woman wants to be with a man who is more powerful in body than the men that her girlfriends are with. *Female jealousy is the greatest aphrodisiac.* Women love making each other jealous in sexual selection. For example, a man who sets up an exciting action date is hitting the base motive of showcasing leadership through stress event but more importantly is he is giving the woman a romantic story to tell her friends. See? When a man is planning a date with a woman he should be thinking "What would be interesting enough that this woman would be proud to share the experience with her girlfriends?" Remember, a woman travels not to see new places as much as she travels to take pictures in front of exotic locale to showcase to other women. FEMALE JEALOUSY. The most common arousal in a woman is trying to steal a man from another woman. A reason for this is that it is low risk thinking based not on individual thought but social proof. The man with a woman or surrounded by woman becomes a safe bet for propagation. But the great reason is that stealing another woman's man will incite sexual jealousy. And being with a man who is wanted by a lot of other women will incite jealousy. Understanding female jealousy is a massive weapon in gaming women. And a man who utilizes a woman's craving for inspiring jealousy in other women will have more success in sexual selection.

This is a major reason that women are attracted to a man's world. It is not necessarily the pleasure of being in the world itself as much as it is about being seen in the world. The woman is on the inside and her girlfriends are on the outside. Women detest boring men not just because these men are not inciting their emotions but rather that these men are not giving them an experience that would make other women jealous. A woman knows the joy she gets in inspiring jealousy in other women is base behavior and non-thinking. It is like an animal lured by scent into a snare. Women will shut off their rational mind and start fighting over a man only because they desire him together. And these women can in truth not care much about the man himself as much as they care about stealing the man from each other. Remember, what has greed can be gamed and female jealousy is a natural greed that women have in our sexual selection. We all can find ourself lured into a trap. But the greed itself is a fascinating feature of female psychology. If a man has ever been around two dogs, he will see greedy behaviors over possessions. Two dogs will fight over something that neither really cares about only because one desires it. This greediness is in us all. But the greed is different between the sexes. For example, a man will have sexual greed in quantity of sexual experience but a woman's greed is revealed in her wanting the possessions of other women. And she will desire to inspire jealousy over her own possessions.

When a man is setting up a date with a woman, he should be thinking "What will give her a story to make her girlfriends jealous?" The more unique the occasion, the more it will allow the woman to say to her friends "My date was special. The guy I am interested in is not mediocre and boring like your men... jealous???"

Let us break this down further by giving an example between two women, one named "Sally" and one named "Betty"

"What did you do last night" Sally asked Betty

"I went out with a guy named Bill. He took me ice skating and then we got drinks afterwards"

Sally flinched but tried not to let Betty know her jealousy. Her man Rick had ordered a pizza and watched sports all night. "That sounds like a fun night" she said with clenched teeth to Betty.

"And then we kissed under a shooting star. It was truly magical" Betty said looking away lost in the good emotion. "In fact, he asked if we want to have a couple's date tonight. He knows an owner of a bar that cooks BBQ on the roof"

Sally grimaced. But she would see how much this Bill truly liked Betty. Sally knew she was prettier than Betty. Betty had mousy features and her hair was always a mess. She was a slob. Sally took care of herself and knew how to actually apply her makeup. Maybe Rick would see that Sally was truly the more beautiful one. "Okay" Sally said to Betty "Lets meet up later" She would wear that tight black dress that she knew got men's looks. The one that pushed up her breast and showed off her legs. She had better legs than Betty. *Why would this guy settle for Betty when he could have a real woman?* Sally thought to herself as Betty talked.

This was a small example. But women know they have this root desire to steal men from each other. They not only want to steal men from each other but want to incite this feeling in other women. And they get great pleasure in having something special that other women do not have. When a man is planning a date with a woman, he should be thinking of that. And the more a man incites this innate feminine greed in his woman of interest the greater her interest will be in him. It is not the bone itself that is attractive to a dog's eye as much as it is the watching eyes of other dogs that makes the bone shine brightest.

Women

crave

winners

     A woman wants a man who is beyond the burden of life. Life is an incredible burden to women because they are born with irrational emotion which causes a great uncertainty of self from their hormone flux. Deep down they understand that they need a man to protect and provide for them. This is why women seek men who make more money and who are showcase strong physical strength. A woman is innately wise to understand that life is only as hard as we are soft. That life has always been difficult from the beginning of time and it will be challenging until the end. Now a woman will not know this consciously but she will understand this on her base level which informs her sexual selection decisioning. But besides making money as provider and weightlifting to build muscles; how can a man project that he is *beyond the burden* of life? A man must project that he is above the common difficulties of other men. He must project that he is not struggling with his own existence. This is one reason that a woman will look upon how well- groomed a man is and how clean he keeps his living conditions. She will observe whether the man is addicted to drugs or alcohol. For example, if a woman goes on a date with a man and his hair is messy, his beard is unkept and his clothes are dirty will signal that the man is drowning in his own reality. This will signal an animal fear in her as he would make a bad protector/provider to her sexual needs in procreation. There are ways a man can project that he is beyond the burden. Start small and make improvements on appearance. Everything is about appearance. Women will say that they just want authentic men who are "Just themselves" but will reward men who overcome themselves. Look in the mirror. What do you see? What can be improved. Fashion has never been my strong point. But to be fair I have always been an intellectual and fashion has seemed superficial. After learning a bit about life, I can say with certainty that fashion is important because women judge men on appearances and so does most the world. We can wish that fashion does not matter but better to accept that it does matter instead of deluding ourselves with this irrational hope. Fashion is personality and status marketing. It helps low risk and low thinking creatures to make safe bets on judging personality. A talented and successful man can dress badly but it would take longer to figure out this man for sexual selection. And women are incredibly skittish and flakey in the beginning stages of sexual selection. Like birds they are easy to take to flight. This is why men who follow women's advice of "Just be yourself" will be easily rejected by women who make their sexual judgments about a man within the first five minutes of meeting him. In those first five, a woman will examine the man more than he thinks she does. She will look at his hair cut/style, how well-groomed he is, how clean he is and what his clothes mean to his financial status. From head to toe. A woman will pull as much information about how a man is "Beyond the burden" in the initial meeting. *Head to toe.* This is why a man should concern himself first with his head and secondly his toe. The best investments a man can make in appealing to women is in how he styles his hair and what shoes he wears. Investing in a quality haircut from a stylist signifies that a man understands style while showing he is well groomed. Next are the shoes. Wearing dirty and cheap shoes signifies to a woman that a man is lacking in style and grooming. Once a man figures out his head and feet then the rest will fall into place. Most people tend to overlook the outfit in favor of head and feet. Why? Because they make a quick glance around the crown of the head and then will spy what shoes a person is wearing. Then they usually stop because the experience requires their attention. But they will make notes of those two. Hair and shoes. Focus on these two key points first and then move onto the rest.

  A woman is a mojo leach. She wants to join a man's self-love and his life that is beyond burden. This is why if a man is living in shabby conditions, does not keep a clean environment and has beer bottles everywhere around his home will signify that the man does not love himself enough for betterment. And that he is sinking in reality rather than rising. This is why a first date at a bar may be just fine but the proceeding dates should not be alcohol based. Choose exciting or wholesome activities that show that the relationship itself will exist inside a bar. See? What world is a woman joining? The dating process is a woman making a decision on what man she is choosing for procreation (Whether she realizes it or not) and what world she will be joining. A man who is exciting, has his life together (Self-improvement focused) and appears beyond the burden of existence will inspire emotion in the woman as she will begin to romanticize the man. She will begin to fantasize about the man who meets her criteria for sexual selection which will create an emotional attachment to him. She will pair bond with him because his world will seem irresistible to her needs. All women want to be beyond the burden of life because all women are imprisoned by their own flesh. Reality is overwhelming to women because their bodies overwhelm them. This is why we have an epidemic of women on anti-depressants and anti-anxiety medications in our feminized times. Too many women are outside masculine frame and they are struggling with their mental health. And masculine frame is the solution to our mental health crisis issue in our civilization. A man who practices masculine frame (As discussed in The Wall Speaks) will give the appearance of mental strength. Frame goes beyond appearance and strengthens a man's own certainty of self which helps him to rationally navigate his leadership of body and mind.

When a woman is looking at a man's profile of self whether online or in person; she will become aroused if a man is beyond the burden of reality. If a man is beyond the burden of sexual selection by being surrounded by women is arousing to other women. If a man is surrounding by male friends will show he is beyond the burden of social anxiety. If a man showcases his expensive car, clothes and shoes will display that he is beyond the burden that so many wallow in. See? A woman is a success hound. Women sexually crave winners and readily give themselves to men who *do not need them*. This is a key thing for a man to understand. There is desperation and there is abundance. The more desperate a man is for a woman the more she will be repelled by him. Neediness is repulsive. And even handsome and wealthy men can repel women with this attitude. Thankfully attitudes can be adjusted. A man's own currency of self can be inflated from his own enforced rarity. For example, a man can be a loser in realty, he can have abundant time on his hands and he can be obsessing over a single woman. But if he is measured in how much attention and validation that he gives the woman will increase her arousal for him. This is why women reward men who know how to distance their true intent. Think about women reward men who ignore them. A woman will message a man and the quicker a man replies back to the woman will be seen as desperate. The woman could be messaging ten different men and she will fantasize about the single man who distances himself most from her. He projects abundance of self-belief and allows the woman to sit in doubt. Doubt is catnip for women in romance. The more a man creates a feeling of doubt on the woman's side the stronger her attachment to him will become. It all falls into the man being beyond the burden of his own desires. A man who can both desire a woman while being above that desire will win the woman. This is why the most sexually thirsty men have the least sex while the men who hide their sexual thirst are the ones having the most sex. These men project that they are beyond the burden of their own flesh which arouses their women. Men who master hiding their true intent are men who will get what they most desire. Women reward mystery. Women reward masculine frames. Women reward the wall that hides intent.

  A man must love himself and he must love his own life before inviting a woman into it. This must be projected through action and not words. A man who loves his life will eat heathy, exercise, dress well, have good hygiene and will not be dependent on alcohol. This is what sexual competition is all about. Many men would rather cling to their weak comforts then pursue women because they have learned to love their decay rather than the embrace of women. Remember, women's sexual arousals in romance make us better men. Our species is strengthened by the elements of attraction in a woman's sexual selection. Women sexually crave men who truly love and take care of themselves. This is not cruel but a love letter that is coded deep in our DNA.

Look before the mirror. Tell yourself you love yourself. Work on becoming successful in body and mind. Project that you are beyond the burden of life. You are worth it. Life is short and gets shorter every day. And female companionship is a great comfort to life. Women and men are meant to be with each other. We complement each other and we work better together than apart. A civilization of single men and single women is a civilization that is falling apart. This is why men must rise to the challenge and increase their sexual pride every day.

A

woman

follows

Women crave to be led. And this means that a man who is wanting to build attraction will need to work on leading conversations. Many feminized men who carry a "We are equals" mindset will fail to focus their mind on leadership. A woman craves to talk about herself but she needs a man to help her feel comfortable in that expression. And this requires a man to provoke thought, listen then keep pushing the conversation forward. Women will let conversations die which breeds uncomfortable silence that kills sexual chemistry. If a man lets a conversation collapse, the woman will feel extreme anxiety during this awkwardness. She will think "This guy is boring" because the man is failing in socializing her properly. A woman will become more passive with a man then with her girlfriends because she is expecting masculine leadership when on dates. *To lead a conversation is to carry the conversation.* And this does not require the woman to be interesting. It only requires the man to make sure that awkward silences rarely if ever happen. Each awkward silence is anti-seductive and makes the woman feel nervous. And this anxiety will make her want to flee. Silence is a form of intimacy that is gained later inside a relationship when two people do not feel they need to save each other from these silences. But in the beginning, silence is death of chemistry. How can a man lead a conversation? He must take a genuine interest in the woman's life without letting it turn into an interview. This requires the man to interject the woman speaking because he wants to add something or require clarification over what is being said. We call this *active listening*. A man who says something provocative will spark opinion in the woman and he can play off that. Do not speak of mundane things like weather or such nonsense. Ask a woman about her day. Then expand on whatever is most interesting. Ask her about her dreams or hope. Ask her what inspires her in life. Ask her questions that bring out her own personalized vision of reality. Then listen, sprinkle in some personal thoughts on what is being discussed and then either switch topics if it is being exhausted or expand it out further. The key thing to remember is to *carry conversation* which means that if the conversation is dying, it is up to the man to switch topic or bring out something that could spark the woman's mind. And do not rush to reply to the woman when she gives her thoughts in the conversation. Hold frame and watch her look at your face for validation. Most times a woman will fade conversation only to pick the conversation back up because the man is holding silence for a brief moment. Replies that are too quick project a neurotic behavior. Holding silence increases a woman's innate neuroticism. This sets the woman into qualification mode. For example, the man will incite the conversation and the woman will give her two cents. But because the man is counting to three or five seconds in silence in his head, the woman will give another two cents to the conversation. Many times, *feminized men will not want the woman to feel three or five seconds of doubt* and so they will swoop into the fill the space which puts them into qualification mode and lowers the sexual chemistry. But having too long of a conversation is anti-seductive. It is feminine frame behavior. If a man is taking a woman on an action date, then they can intercut the action with some conversation. This allows the woman to feel connected with the man regardless if they are talking the whole time. It allows her to fuel her imagination on what is not being said. She feels his energy under his leadership and that is enough most times to secure sexual selection. The more action on the date the less talk is required. But it is important to at least bring up one personal or deep topic that makes the woman feel connected emotionally. A couple can be rock climbing and during a short break the man asks "What is a dream that is important to you?" - Then the woman says it and they are back into the action. This may be enough to raise her attraction just because he sparked her mind and imagination. And even if a man can carry a conversation on a date, it is best that he cuts the date relatively short. It is best to allow room for mystery and fantasy. And a conversation that goes overly long kills mystery. At that point it is best to ask the woman if she wants to go to a second location or just wrap the date up right there. And do not say "I had a good time" - Many feminized men do this to make their intentions known and to reassure the woman. It is best to allow the woman to hold some doubt which fuels her erotic mystery. Just give her a smile and say "I'll message you. Take care" - What intent can be made of that? Not much. Do you see? This is why it is important not to say "I really like you. I had a great time. We will have to do this again" See? That is cornball behavior that is anti-seductive.

But let us rewind a bit. A man should not be having long messages with a woman prior or after a date. If a man approaches a woman and gets her number, he should communicate to give direction for a date. Most messaging kills mystery and deflates sexual chemistry. Do not give her daily messages about "How is your day going?" or such nonsense. Be direct, concise and give direction. Then after a date be the same way. Only communicate to give direction on the next date. And it is best to wait a while to let the woman grind her wheels in doubt about the man's feelings. A woman grinding in anxiety and doubt over a man's unknown feelings is seductive. This is why feminized men who are quick to reassure women and make their every intent known deflate their own sexual chemistry with them. A framed man knows that emotions are important to women and emotions must be played with to heighten arousal. From the first interaction with a woman to the last, always be leading. Women expect men not just to carry frame but to also carry conversation. And then once an emotional attachment is formed a man can relax a little. This is when women begin to over communicate to reassure themselves of emotional validation with the men they are attached to. But the beginning requires more effort in conversation because the attachment has yet to form for the woman to hustle in her own need for validation.

The

eyes

command

When a man is talking to a woman, his eyes will either draw her into his frame or repel her. What does it mean to have leader's eyes? It means being able to command and lead others eyes into observance. *Women will be the first to mention equal distribution and the last to reward it with their behaviors.* A man who gives equal eye contact with a woman will be punished rather than rewarded by this equal mindset. Why? Because a woman wants to bear the child of a leader. She wants to be commanded, directed and possessed by a masculine authority. And what does it mean to project authority with the eyes? It means to recognize the inequal distribution of eye contact that fuels arousal.

Let us break down how eye contact can be altered to pull a woman into sexual interest. Inside the brain there is a group of cells called "Mirror neurons" that are mostly collected in the part of the brain called Broca's area. A Princeton University study found that people who are more empathetic have more activity in this region. A study by James W. Pennebaker concluded that language style matching increased when a participant was speaking to a distracted partner. What was the distraction? The distracted partner was asked to do a math task while in conversation. And the less distracted participant began to match their verbal style with the multitasker and both ended up reported liking each other more than two undistracted participants. What is the rationale behind something like this? It is that we are coded to mold ourselves to those who display leadership qualities. And a leadership quality is distraction because leaders are mentally burdened with thinking beyond the moment. This is why a man who acts distracted from a woman's presence will pull her attention to him.

There is a Benjamin Franklin quote of "When you speak to a man, look on his eyes; when he speaks to you, look upon his mouth" – There is deep wisdom to this. Looking upon the eyes is falling into the frame of the person. It is follower behavior and projects neediness of validation. When a man looks slightly off from the eyes of the person talking is a slight distraction that takes the pressure of performance off the speaker while allowing mirror neurons to fire off from the distracted attention.

When a man is speaking to a woman he should focus on the center of her eyes. This is a commanding gesture. A woman will be caught in the dominant gaze and will surrender her frame to this. Think about the eyes as both windows to the soul but also spotlights of attention. A woman craves to look into eyes because this allows her to use her feminine intuition to unpack the man while giving her the attention of a commanding presence which is sexually arousing to her. Dual effect.

Another key thing with about eye contact is knowing when to look away from speaking. Looking directly in the eyes the entire time is not charismatic. We can take snapshots of key moments in a discussion when we make a small laugh/small smirk, "Capture the eye" of the observer and look away. This will pull the observer along to where we turn/look away which is a psychological leash of interest.

The eyes are important in regards to gauging a woman's mental health. Women with wide eyes where the whites surround the iris are manic in their expression. They do not have the measured closure of lid that is a sign of measured reasoning. And a woman who looks up and to the side while speaking has severe mental issues. These eye positionings should be omitted from a man's own behavior. Keep the lids measured in closure and not wide eyed in confusion. Frame is mystery and discipline. Even the eyes must be disciplined. The lids are like curtains that a woman wants to look past in order to see what is backstage. Women love men who know how to keep the lids in control just like women love men who know how to smirk instead of grin. It is bodily control and framed behavior. Micro expressions that show authority of self. And this authority of self is a frame of thought. A man sets the frame of thought for the woman to join.

A man who cannot look a woman in the eyes while he is speaking is showing that he gets nervous when commanding others. And a man who overly looks a woman in her eyes when she is speaking is giving her too much authority. The eyes are crucial in building arousal and showing strong sense of self. And a man who is not beholden to a woman's eyes when she is speaking will trigger her mirror neurons thereby pulling her into his frame.

When a man is first showing romantic interest in a woman on approach, he should lock eyes with her and make a small smile. The woman should be the first to look away from the man. Why? This is dominant possession. A man is owning the space between them and he is taking ownership of the woman's gaze. Men who break eye line first are men who are projecting weakness to women in approach. The eye is the projected authority from a distance between two individuals. And a man who shows he can command that space with direct eye contact shows that he can offer the woman masculine leadership. Women crave to be dominated and lead by men. And a man cannot handle eye contact with a woman is a man who has not learned the power of his own authority. Many fatherless men have issues with eye contact because their sense of self is in doubt and they become reactionary to the feeling they receive from the gazes of others. Why? Because eye contract makes us self-aware. And that self-awareness is like a someone looking in the window of our home. What do they see? How does that make us feel? Are we unmoved and proud? Or do we crumble in the spotlight of attention? What does it take to be a leader? To stand tall before the many. All their eyes gazing on one individual. He gazes out and over them all. Not fazed by their eyes. Leadership requires eye mastery. And eye mastery takes tremendous belief in self. But it is not simply believing self as much as it is in disbelieving others. See? *To lead a group is to believe the self over the group which requires disbelief in them leading themselves.* This is how a man should be with a woman. He is assuming authority over her and leads her with his eye contact. He pulls her in with commanding eyes when he is speaking and again pulls her in by removing his gaze from her eyes when she is speaking. A dance between the sexes through sight.

A

man

unlike

the

others

The key thing for a man to realize in sexual selection is that women by in large do not judge a man individually. They judge men with a hive mind through group consensus. This is why women will fantasize and crush over the same man. It is not that the man himself is something truly special as much as it is about sexual competition being stimulated. And that group decisioning increases the desire of a woman and her peers. This is what a man should consider when plotting the early stages of romance. A woman wants a man to make her girlfriends jealous. And this requires a man to give a woman an experience that is worth talking about. There is a song by Bonnie Raitt called "Something to talk about" – It perfectly encapsulates a woman's mind in romance. She wants to be able to brag (Even in a low key way) about her romantic experiences. When a man is planning a date idea with a woman he is interested in, he should be thinking "This will give the woman a story to tell" – A woman will have fun on a date but it is the act of telling her friends about it that secures her emotions to the man. Women build emotion not just by experiencing emotion with a man as much as during the moments of sexual competition with their peers. They want to be with someone doing something that would make their peers envious. Girls just want to have fun and they just want to rub that fun in their friends faces. Did a woman enjoy a date rock-climbing or did she more enjoy being able to tell her friends that she had an adventurous date? See? It is about the story and not the experience itself. When a woman has fun with a man, what she truly is getting aroused by is that her friends are unhappy that she is having fun. A woman's arousal is filtered through feminine competition and jealousy. But women do get excited on adventure dates because they are all erogenous zones covering eggs that enjoy leaving the nest. They are used to sitting arounds and gabbing about other people's lives. So when they are exposed to something that is worth gabbing about they get excited and aroused. Inside their mind they think "This will get them talking. This will make them jealous" – This is why a man should be thinking of not necessarily doing something truly fun as he must be thinking of doing something that will be worth talking about. *It is not about the moment as it is about the reflection of the moment.* Women do not love traveling, they love showing pictures and talking of their travels. It is the display that matters more than experience. A woman will not be "In the moment" during adventures as much as she is plotting/planning how she can market the moment to inspire jealousy. That is why doing something novel will end up being a positive regardless of actual enjoyment in the novel experience. Women are story collectors. They are disconnected to experience and merely play act during new experience while thinking of the end goal of telling others about the experience. If a man wants to be clever, he could see what his woman's friends care about. And then he can figure out a date that would make them drool in envy. This will incite sexual competition and increase the emotional attraction to himself. It is not good enough to game a woman, a man must game her entire social group. Women become aroused through each other. They are not individuals like men. They are connected to each other through a hive mind. Incite the hive to incite her heart. A man could do something romantic in front of a woman's friends while incorporating them into the romance for mass effect. It is not about one woman's heart, it is about a woman's friends' eyes and ears. There is an ultimatum game about "Would you rather this scenario of decadent luxury with no memory or ...." - A woman would only choose the memory option because the memory is what gains a woman the most satisfaction because the memory itself is used as bait to inflict negative emotion on her peers. Note that. Inflict negative emotion on peers. And what does a woman say to a friend that she is displaying happiness for? "I am so jealous of you!" - She is giving her friend what she wants by being vocal about it. Women love making each other jealous and this stirs their emotions which fuels their own sexual selection. In a way, a woman is like a dog that drags a bone into the center of a room to chew on it in front of other dogs. The enjoyment of the bone is fueled by the greedy competition and inspiration of envy. All groups of women will have one standard crush they will all discuss in lust over. They love fighting over the bone of their affections. They set themselves up as a harem on their own accord. "He is cute" a woman will say. And the other women see that a man is being desired which fuels their interest in him. It is a domino effect of passion that first starts with one woman's interest in a man that pulls the other women into greed. It is greed that compels a woman forward in romance and it is greed that makes a woman like an animal to be gamed. It is greed that is good in romance. This is why a man who wants to be good with women should be focused on inspiring their greed. It is a greedy heart that falls in love. A woman would never allow herself to fall in love for charity. There must be meat on the bone of her desires to feast on before her feminine peers. This is why when a man is plotting date ideas with a woman, he should be thinking about giving a story to inspire greed in her friends. Think adventure and think novelty. Make the experience special and this will give the woman something special to sell. When a man plans a mundane date idea, the woman is dreading having to tell her friends about the mundane experience. It is the opposite effect of inspiring jealousy. It is inspiring pity from her peers and making a woman feel invisible. Women know that mediocrity is invisibility. It is the truth of reality. And a woman's worst nightmare is to be invisible in her social circle. Her worst fear is to be the one lusting in jealousy over another woman. This is one key reason that women hate boring men. It sets them up as the jealous one while making them invisible before others. And this is a big reason that women will dismiss men who approach with boring pick-up lines. It makes them dread the upcoming boring experience. Women love novelty because novelty can be sold through story. And they always talk about their romantic lives with each other "This guy used this pick-up line" a woman will say to her friend "That is a new one" her friend might say. "He took me on a unique date" She will tell her friend who is trying not to appear jealous "My man just watched tv all night" – In her mind she knows she is winning. She is living a life and her friend is wishing she was her. This is feminine consciousness in sexual selection and it has been this way ever since the beginning and will be this way until the very end.

A

woman

is

without

a

world

Women are homeless in spirit and seek to be under a man's frame. But what kind of frame do they seek? What kind of world do they want to join? This is what a man must realize about women. They do not seek a man who joins their world, they seek a man's world to join. They seek to join a man's world that is beyond the burden of reality. It is the world beyond burden that most appeals to women. A return to Eden. Just as they collect pillows for sofas, they seek to be relieved of the burden of reality. Women are comfort obsessed because women are bound by flesh to harsh reality. Their bodies deform from childbirth and they are reminded of this transfiguration by monthly blood loss through their legs. Reality is brutal but especially to women who doubt their own sense of self. This hormone flux spirals their irrationality as they are conflicted in decision. Note that. Sense of self. A woman is a doubter of self and seeks a strong sense of self to align herself to. Women are collectivist to groupthink because they regulate their sense of self through group conformity. Conforming makes them feel reassured of their sense of self. And this is why women seek strong willed men who have sense of self like steel to associate their own identity to. A woman will conform her entire being around a strong-willed man. It is her nature. And what makes up a strong-willed man? His sense of self is complete and not reliant on group pressure. He is the pressure over the group and not the reverse. This is catnip to pussy. They crave to be dominated by the certainty of self that comes with strong frame. They are reassured emotionally by the certainty of framed men. Women are mojo leaches and psychic vampires feeding on the vibrations of frame. This is where many men go astray because many men are weak willed and ruled by doubt. These men wilt before group pressure and easily doubt themselves when confronted with a different view of realty. To be certain of self is to rise about groupthink that controls others. And it is not just certainty that women sexually crave. It is the world of a man that a woman craves. She craves to be inside the worldview of her man. She craves to be fed the energy of a man who loves his life. It is the love of life that women crave in men. A man must love his life completely and be inspired. He must romanticize himself. He must have swagger in his sexual pride. His sexual pride must drip off his being. And how does a man get to this state? It is a worldview that creates a world. It is one step over the other that allows us to climb the mountain of our hopes and dreams. We set the frame of thought for others to think inside. We create the game for others to play. We shape reality to our own will. Look yourself in the mirror and what do you see? How much sex do you see staring back at you? Take yourself seriously but learn to bend in charisma to those seeking to humiliate your image. Believe in the power of sexual pride. It is this sexual pride that fills the empty vessel of a woman's arousal. A woman craves to align herself with pride. A woman wants to align herself with fun. A woman wants to align herself with power. See? Women seek association with what helps them overcome the burden of their own existence. For a man to be attractive to a woman, first he must be attractive to himself. Before a woman desires a man, he must first desire his own reality. Many men will go on dates with woman while carrying tremendous self-doubt, disbelief and fear. Of course this would repel these women. We must prize our seed over the woman's egg. This is the reverse by nature but we can alter by sheer will of frame. If a man believes his seed is more precious than his woman's egg, she will join him in that frame of thought. And why would a man prize his seed so highly? Because there is no other choice. We live short and brutal lives that end in death. This is the reality of existence. And that is why it is key that we summon belief and optimism over our short reality. It will soon end and this is why we must enjoy it. This frame of thought is contagious and pulls women in. What kind of men do women seek? Men who seize life. Men who love life. Men who take pride in themselves. This is powerful energy that exudes from these men that women pick up like hounds over a scent. A woman wants to love life but she knows she must love life through the frame of a man's self-reference. Her doubt is cured by his certainty. Her boredom is cured by his adventure. Her self-loathing is cured by his self-belief.

What does it mean to have strong sense of self? It means to emotionally validate the self and to remain unphased by others doubt in that self. Let us breakdown emotional validation of self. It means to be sure of the inner voice within one's head. And to strengthen the voice is to know the voice separated from others. This voice strengthening can come through a practice of solitude. Our inner voice when alone must grow louder in its own sense of reality by being deprived on external validation. The aspect of being unphased by others judgment is a strong attractant to women. They are innately phased by others because they use others for their own emotional regulation. And how can a man remain unphased? Understand the reality of frames. Understand that others want to place their frame over you and that they want to flip your frame. This comes through dominance tactics and shit tests. When a man is subservient to others dominate frame is signaling self-doubt just as when a man becomes reactive to others testing of his frame is proof, he is in doubt over himself. A frame must be strong and stable. Understanding tactics as described in my books is helpful but what is more helpful is to believe the self to such a high degree that doubting others realities becomes natural. Think about the self like a body before God's light and others are merely shadows from the body's form. What does it mean to be tested by a shadow? There is no weight to it and this is how a man passes tests. Think about the self in a spotlight on a stage and everyone else is supporting actors to your performance. This is romanticization of self. A man who becomes ego centric allows a woman to form her own ego around him. She draws belief from his self-belief. We create believers and we create doubters. It is though our own frame of thought and our presentation of that thought. A woman will fall in love with a man who is already in love with himself. And this is not proven by weak speech of "I love myself" – This would prove doubt of self because it is waiting on external validation for approval. Self-love moves in silence and certainty of behavior. This is what women call when a man is "smooth" or has "swagger" – His every movement projects that he has strong sense of self and does not let others doubt affect him. This swagger pulls women in because they too want to share his confidence of self. They too want to overcome their innate self-doubt by joining his supreme confidence. Women love confident men because women are innately doubt filled. They seek this opposite in order to feel completed. We are compliments to each other once we understand the polarity between the sexes. A woman is herself and a man must overcome himself. He must project that he is beyond the burden of reality by projecting supreme confidence over his own reality.

When a man is texting, he should text back in at least 4/3 time women texts. This allows the woman to be the one to close the distance. It allows her to close the emotional gap on her own without the man displaying emotional neediness by closing the gap himself. It shows that he is desperate, has too much time on his hands and needs emotional validation. Women crave masculine leaders and leaders are busy. This is fine measurement of pleasure for women. They like to be teased sexually. They like to be the one chasing affection because it helps them to fall into their feminine pleasure. But a man who messages back or shows his affection too early is like a man stumbling in the dance of love over his woman's feet. It is clumsy and dull behavior that deflates female attraction. Women love dance and men who can lead in dancing because women crave to be led in order. They crave a man who can finely measure himself out. They crave men who do not depend on them for emotional support. Men who communicate with at more or faster than a woman are the ones chasing which flips the power to the woman's side which ruins sexual chemistry. Think about the steps of romance. A man makes an introduction in approach which creates energy and mystery. He exits and lets space grow. He lets mystery grow. Men who kill their own mysteries are like men who trip in fall while holding a woman in a dance. Goofy footed lovers kill romance. Give the woman some space to grow in affection. Absence makes the heart fonder because it allows a woman to pine for her lover. See? To pine we must have distance. It is the measured out emotional distance that allows emotion to grow. When a man closes the gap too quickly with a woman is like a hunter stomping towards game. Women get spooked and go into flight. This is a major reason men get frustrated in sexual selection. They do not realize the basic steps to take in the initial stages of romance. It takes fine discipline in building the beginnings of emotion in a woman. It takes discipline to incite arousal in a woman. Sloppy and undisciplined behavior ruins this attraction. Men fail in romance not just from ignorance but from laziness. It is easy to say "Maybe she is not like the others" or more apt "Maybe she does not mind sloppy dance moves in romance" See? It is putting more of an expectation on the woman to overlook the behavior of the man who should be rising above with her needs. Or it is saying "This woman does not care that I'm desperate because she is desperate" What a way to live. Truly. Have pride in the steps of arousal. A woman is an emotional instrument that leads our dance. We play her and she makes us want to step. Take the lead by displaying leadership qualities. And a leader should not be overly available or in constant need of emotional validation. Be strong. Give her distance so feelings can grow. Remember, feelings grow not just in the act of being around a woman but in the absences of that time. This takes strong inner fortitude to overcome this behavior. Do not give up. And if you fail with one woman just look for another. To say "This was THE ONE AND ONLY" is to be in a beggar's mindset and it is a curse on the consciousness. Women are in abundance. In fact, there are more women in most populations because men die earlier for various reasons. Do not kick yourself too hard for letting one get away. Get back out there and start learning the moves. And you will see the finely measured steps pull them in instead of scaring them off.

Steady

the

aim

Sexual selection for men can be emotionally exhausting and frustrating to our egos. High rejection is the standard for men in sexual selection. This is why I encourage men to spread out their aim towards multiple women at one time. Because it is common for one woman to reject or flake during the early stages. If one drops out for any reason there is another to focus on. But more important than multiple aims is to stead the aim of each. Sexual selection is incredibly challenging for men and this requires us to emotional detach in order to not become disheartened. Spread the aim and then do not let rejection hurt the ego. This will be a challenge at first but with practice becomes easier. Remember life and sexual selection is all math. It is all algorithms. And instead of thinking "I am pathetic" Or becoming emotionally hurt by rejection; detach and think rationally "What adjustment in my behavior do I need to reconfigure?" Because the same woman that rejected a man would have accepted him in an altered scenario. Altering presentation should be a man's concern in the process of love. For example, if a woman agrees to give her number is proof that she sees potential in the man. It is then on him to screw up that opportunity from that point on. And if a woman agrees to meet a man on a date, it is on him to ruin that date from the beginning of the meeting. The same for if a woman agrees to go home with a man. It is on him to mess it up. After an initial attraction is shown, it is the continued presentation of self that ruins a man's chances at romance. Many men take sexual rejection and women flaking on them personally which hurts them. And what does that hurt do? It disheartens them which can make them opt out of sexual competition. Opting out of sexual competition is lacking sexual pride. We must protect our pride as men and we must overcome ourselves. If a man just followed a woman's advice of "Just be yourself" then a man would be stumbling in failure without learning how to improve. We overcome ourselves which means we alter our configurations. What is the self? *The self is a constant improvement on the configuration of our behavior.* That is the self. The self is whatever helps you to succeed in life and love. Nothing is stagnant in our being. Failing is not truth. The truth is winning. The truth is success. And women have tremendous amount of power in the early stages of romance. But that power flips eventually when the woman becomes emotionally attached. That is when a man's hard work pays off. But to secure emotional attachment in a woman requires deep emotional detachment during the process for a man. A feminized man will think "I will just fantasize and focus on this single woman" But when she rejects him; he becomes crushed in spirit. This is like seeing a hunter missing one target and then retiring for a long period to recuperate his loss. It is a goddamn waste of time and a waste of emotional energy. Learn phrases to detach from failed experience like "It is what it is" – This is what we say when we miss a shot but must focus on making another. See? It is not about failed shots as much as it is about us regaining our confidence for the next shot. And when we emotionally invest too much energy in one woman, then we will lose confidence when we should be regaining confidence. Think. A man gets a woman's number and he texts her back too quickly which causes her to lose interest. Should he let it hurt him or should he just think "My fault. I should have applied the 4/3 time rule and the 2/3 speech rule" See? It is just math to build romantic interests and has less to do with the true person of a man's heart. A woman will think "This guy is a loser" when she rejects/flakes on him. And she is right but it is not personal. He is a loser because he is not using a winning strategy. When a man starts mastering game is when the commonality of women opens up before him. Women become less personal in romance which allows him to detach from the experience. And the key thing for a man to remember is that there is always a woman for him to attempt a new strategy upon. Just say "It is what it is" and move on. Emotionally move on. Do not let it touch the ego. A failed shot is not representative of the self but giving up a future shot is. Failure is opportunity for a new strategy. And strategizing is life. Men who are good with women are men who have failed many times with women. This high failure rate allows them reconfiguration of presentation. "That failed. Maybe this will work" – Do not give up and quit just because sexual selection is difficult. The most difficult games are the most satisfying to master. Learn winning strategies and abandon failed strategies. This is what is means to be a man. And this is the true self.

Building

the

cage

of

love

A woman does not fall in love with a man, she falls in love with his presentation of self. And this presentation of self represents a world that she wants to join. The man must love his world for his woman to want to join it. This is called *sharing frame of thought.* A man sets the thought for the woman to join. Men who are burdened by reality and unhappy with their lives repel women. This is why summoning self-belief is essential in romance. And how can a man summon self-belief. He must perform acts of discipline to increase that belief in his spirit. This will project his self-love like a scent under the woman's nose. She will follow this self-love into the cage of love. She will be bound in emotional attachment to this self-love. Let us go into how acts of discipline increase self-belief which enhances self-love.

When we master ourselves, we increase the power of belief. To push away indulgence is a great act of belief. Why? Because this tells our subconscious that we believe enough in tomorrow to sacrifice for today. The more we can summon power over our self during a day will push self-love to tomorrow. The world seems more challenging the less we are disciplined. If acts of discipline are acts of belief, then being undisciplined in indulgences are acts of disbelief. And the more we commit acts of disbelief the more we lose sense our own self. This weakened state is like soft hands in a hard world. The pain of having to deal with reality will feel too much to bear only because the callous is missing. A man must become harder than life. We must strive for self-belief daily. And this requires us to make positive changes of discipline with consistency. Each man has different weaknesses but let us take my own for example. If I have an alcoholic drink, the desire for another drink will overwhelm me. The reason for this goes beyond a genetic inclination towards alcoholism and is a relief from the obsessive thinking I am prone to. It is incredibly challenging to shut off my hyper thinking. But when I choose the alcoholic indulgence other positive behaviors will drop away. This could be eating healthy or going to the gym. And then before I know it a dependency to alcohol will form over days of indulgence while my good habits begin to disappear. This dependency is disbelief in self. And the more I depend on alcohol to ease my existential suffering the more I will feel lost without that dependency. When our indulgences replace healthy habits is like us digging ourselves into a hole of disbelief. And from that hole the world will seem darker and the fear inside ourselves will begin to overwhelm us. This dark state of mind comes from our actions of disbelief. The more we place our belief on external indulgence the more we atrophy our internal fortitude which exists to help us emotionally handle the stress of reality. And sexual selection is a massive stress that requires strong self-belief.

Think about internal fortitude as steel beams in a sky scraper. The more we commit acts of discipline the more reinforced our skyscraper of self will become. But when we forsake discipline for indulgence, we are weakening the structure of the skyscraper of self. When we overly depend on indulgence is a decay in the structure of our sense of identity. An alcoholic will lose his sense of self because his sense of self will depend on alcohol. A man who externalizes his self-belief away from himself will atrophy in his internal self-belief. Sobriety and discipline are powerful reinforcements of sense of self. Women are drawn to men with strong sense of self. And a man who controls his diet and disciplines his body will appear strong. But that is merely a display of his strong internal fortitude that women truly crave. It is an easy way for a woman to see whether or not a man is strengthening his self through acts of discipline.

To strengthen self, we must venture through a void of doubt and pain. Why? Because to give up indulgence is to be left in a place of anxiety and pain. What does it mean for a man who is used to eating sugar snacks every day to give them up? It means he has two battlefronts. He has to battle the uneasy feelings that come with blood sugar as well as battling the feelings of being without his weak-willed reward. And this is why most people live undisciplined lives. They seek the short-term boost to their sense of self because they do not have the strength to believe in tomorrow. To believe in the future self is to have a spirit of abundance. And this abundant mindset will project out from a man. He will pull women into his orbit because he loves himself to such a degree that he does not need weak willed indulgences to believe in his life. An obese man is not just physically repulsive to a woman because of the superficiality of fat alone but rather because the obesity is a physical manifestation that the man lacks self-belief. The more a man is dependent on weak willed indulgences the more in a state of decay he will be. He is sinking in realty and is giving himself belief boosters. Why would a woman want to join that decay? Why would a woman to join that disbelief in reality? Why would a woman want to join a man's world if his sense of self is weak? This is why a man must summon the power for small changes in his life. He must start mastering his own realty. Strengthen his self-belief through acts of discipline.

A

strong

sense

of

self

The greatest aphrodisiac to a woman is power. A man who has power over himself and others reassures a woman of her innate fear and doubt of self. Women crave strong psyches in men above all else. And this strong sense of self pulls them into frame. How can a man increase the power of himself? He must see it as a role he is fulfilling. When a man goes on a date with a woman he should become like a doctor of love. This is a cliché roleplay for sex. A man who plays doctor with a woman is a man who plays strong frame with a woman. Women by in large love going to doctors and therapists because women by in large love being reassured by frame. They seek authorities to reassure them of their fear and doubt. This is why a man should assume this authority role from the start of the date. He has the certainty of authority like doctor to patient. He is leading the conversation like doctor to patient. The same for a psychologist to patient. It is the frame of authority that reassures women. And this frame of authority can be had just by will alone but is most optimal with intelligence. This is why it is crucial for men to read books.

Reading books does multiple positive things in romance. It strengthens the inner voice by listening to the strong voice of a writer. The key is to find writers with strong voices and not just read brain candy. Reading books is a slow discipline that slows a man's behaviors. It is a meditative activity that increases intelligence while slowing behavior for power projection. Many positive things in romance are gained by reading books. And intelligence is a frame flipper. Even the most dominant types have to be careful around the intelligent because power shifts with intellectual superiority. A man who reads anything that has real world merit or seriousness will assume authority through his literary interests. Reading books helps with game.

      Solitude also strengthens the inner voice. To be alone with the inner voice is to strengthen the inner voice. To be separate from the collective is to grow in individualism. And to be individualistic is anti-feminine. Individualistic men have strong sense of selves which allows them to doubt the many in order to LEAD them. See? A man who reads and spends times alone is conditioning himself for leadership. It is crucial for a man to love himself to such a high degree that he finds comfort in being alone. Being a leader is a lonely experience. It is lonely on the top. And this is why a man must not doubt himself when he is in solitude. He must build and strengthen his psyche by empowering his internal fortitude. He must separate his consciousness from groupthink in order to rise about them in authority. This will sharpen a man's psyche and strengthen his view of realty. The power of his frame will encapsulate the woman like a doctor or psychologist. She will be reassured by the strength of his frame which will help her to submit under it. Remember, framed men do not force submission, they inspire it through strength of frame. Take time for yourself and improve the individual spirit through reading in solitude. Grow strong in the inner voice and the outer projection will exude authority.

Hiding

sexual

intent

Nothing spooks the birds more than clumsy steps. And nothing scares women away more than sexual desperation from men. A man must be beyond the burden of his own physical desires. Women are surrounded by desperate men's sexual thirst. These women are sexually eyed by the mediocre masses of men. And women are overwhelmed by men's sexuality in dating. A woman becomes emotionally attached to a man during sex. This is one reason why women are careful about being penetrated. Also, women have more at stake during sex since they are burdened by the decision in body. All this makes women especially sexually cautious doing the initial stages of sexual selection. When a man is displaying his sexual desires with a woman on the first moments will most times scare the woman away. The sex must be hidden inside frame. We conceal our intent which fuels the desires. To hold back creates flames of desire while showcasing that we are beyond the burden of the mediocre masses. Concealing sexual intent is seductive. A woman loves mystery. And a man who does not play by the same sexually thirsty rules of other men will incite her erotic imagination. This does not mean a man is not sexual at all. It is that the sexuality goes underground and is inflamed by suppression. Something as simple as hand holding becomes sexual when the intent is concealed. When we control the passion, it becomes stronger. And nothing deflates sexual passion more than explaining it through speech. Hidden intent. Sex is better the less we talk about it just like a joke is better when not explained. A man should be leading a woman on a date with conversation and introduction of touch. Most women paint their nails not just to look pretty but to give men an excuse to hold their hands. Place her hand in your own hand and comment on the nails. This is dating basics that introduces touch while not being overtly sexual. And while a man is holding his woman's hands in his own, he can then continue talking. Touch therefore becomes background to the conversation. This will make her think about the comfort of touching in the background of the interaction. If a couple are on a walking date, it is key for the man to take the woman's hand. This does two things. It shows leadership as the man is leading the woman by the hand while conditioning her to be comfortable to his touch. In our times where sex is overwhelmingly pornographic and vulgar; something as simple as non-sexual touch will inflate sexual feeling. Why? Because to hold back passion is to fuel passion. It is through non sexual touch on a date that sex is thought about. A touch on the hand, arm or leg in conversation is building attraction. It is a form of boldness in transcending the space between a man and woman. A domination of the body through physical touch. We do not just touch anybody. Touch is sacred. And this small touching behavior is setting the frame of sexuality. One reason that first dates die from lack of chemistry is that the man is not being bold enough in his physicality. He must establish that this is a romantic occasion and not just an occasion between two friends. But the key thing is to hide sexual intent by being non sexual in touch. This is why hand holding and hand touching are both key things to do on the first date. By the time the date is over and the man is going to go in for a kiss; the physical precedent has already been set. The woman has become familiar with touch and she has fallen into the romantic frame set by the man. Women know men want sex and a man who has the power to hide his sex only increases desire. A man who is countering his primal urges will incite mystery. And a woman wants to know what makes this man different. And what makes him different? He is hiding his intent well. He lays out the seductive bait and waits for the woman to feel comfortable before she is trapped in passion.

But sex is not just emotional with women. It also is ego investment. For example, the more physical a man becomes with a woman the more she will defend his worth because he has incorporated his worth with her. How? A woman holds herself in high esteem and so if she allowed a man to get physical with her then he must have worth. It is backwards thinking. Women will view men as mediocre in worth until the men boldly dominate the women physically which alters the woman's views because the woman does not want to be associated with a loser. And so a woman will rewrite the man's narrative after he boldly interacts with her in order to spare her own ego. This is why a woman will be lukewarm with a man until after she has sex with him. Then she will flip to chasing him not just from emotional attachment but ego preservation. Bold men alter paradigms in consciousness. And timid men remain in the lukewarm waters of the friendzone only because they refuse to understand the rules of sexual selection. A woman will think a man a loser and then think him a winner after he gets sex only because her ego must be protected over her decisions. And that ego preservation allows her to emotionally invest. It is the ego first and emotion second. Most talk about women and their emotion attachment while skipping over what leads to that emotion. It is the ego preservation that writes the romantic narrative after the fact.

When a man acts bold in his physical dominance with a woman, she either rejects him outright or submits to his will. And if a man warmed a woman up with small non sexual touch, then she will be more apt to surrender to sexual touch when it comes.

But one thing a man may encounter with a woman is her professing virtue while rejecting the advancement of sexual touch. For example, a woman may say a soft "no" when a man gets physical. This is different than a hard "NO" - Why? Because the soft no is usually an act that is showcasing virtue/innocence while still desiring the physicality. The hard NO is rejecting the physicality altogether from lack of desire. Let me be clear as day, I am not saying to ignore a woman's sexual rejection. But what I am saying is that women do have multiple reasons for saying "No" during sexual interaction and not all of them are meant to stop the interaction but merely to showcase virtue before the act. When a man is first learning a woman, he will notice that no sometimes means yes. This comes from maturity and age. But only have becoming more experience. Do not think that I am giving you permission to rape women. Rape is horrible and unframed. What I am saying is that women use language in a subtle way and not a direct way. This takes individual discernment that is based on the woman and sexual chemistry of situation. Do not blame me for speaking truth. Your decision is yours alone to bear. To be a man is to bear the responsibility of all things. But just be aware that women use the word "No" with different meanings and not necessarily to stop the interaction but rather to shrug responsibility for the interaction. See? This is why most women profess virtue while surrendering to less than virtuous acts. Also let me be clear as day on another issue, I am not encouraging promiscuous behavior. We must discuss the common behaviorism of women to better help men in their sexual selection. And that requires honesty about how women act in physical situations.

The

language

of

love

How a man uses his words is essential in building attracting with a woman. There are multiple facets to this. The first point we will discuss is agreeable speech. This is disingenuous and is anti-seductive. It is the language of toothless niceness that is devoid of personality. A woman will say/message something and a man will say "That is cool" or "Wow. I like that" This is the dread inducing language that is like nails on a chalkboard for women to endure. It is boring speech that deflates attraction. There is a saying that goes "If you do not have anything nice to say, do not say anything at all" - This saying is anti-seductive when dealing with women. Women are not seeking agreeably boring men to say nice nothings to them. It is boring, does not provoke emotion and displays no leadership. A man does not need to respond to a woman with "Nice nothings" - He can provoke or ignore. If a woman says something, challenge her a little or ignore her and move the discussion somewhere else. Do not kill the energy with saying nice nothings.

Another language point is setting up qualification mode through conversation. When asking questions such as "What are some talents you have?" - The woman is in the spotlight and must tap dance for approval. When she mentions something, sit back and say "Not bad"— "That is pretty good" Remember to never give overwhelming praise but rather give slight praise. This spikes conflicted emotion by lifting up the qualification in a cloud of doubt. It leaves room for improvement. Another is "You are a good kisser. I give you a 7.5/10. We can work on improving it" See? The man must position himself as the authority that is pleased by the woman and not the reverse. Setting the frame of authority in the first date is essential. The man as leader and the woman as follower. When the man speaks, he is setting up scenarios where the woman must think about how she is qualifying to the man. A man leads a woman by the hand, leads her in conversation and then leads her thoughts through his use of language. Supreme manipulations that wet the palate of desire.

Another point is to avoid too much conversation. Remember to get the woman to talk 2/3s of the time. The more a man speaks the more he falls into anxious qualification to the woman. A woman will fall back and just let a man spin his wheels in conversation which sets the woman up as authority to dismiss or approve. This makes the man "tap dance" for attention. It is anti-seductive to talk more than the woman. And it is anti-seductive to make the dates themselves all about talking. A first date can be focused on talking because it is the initial introduction (As long as woman is talking more) but the dating experience should be about leading the woman through a non-talking experience. Feminized men think the best way to increase passion in a woman is through talking to her. But this is false. The best way for a man to increase passion in a woman is by allowing her to talk, feel listened to and to lead her with frame through an event. It can be as simple as talking briefly over a coffee and then going on a walk somewhere where the visuals can be discussed. This requires little money and the woman will enjoy the experience. What feminized men do not realize is how little talking is needed for romance. Hell, two people can fall in love while barely knowing each other's language. This happens every day. Sexual attraction requires very little talking. All it requires is that there is flirting, frame and leadership.

Another point is avoiding all self-deprecating language and complaining on the date. Many men will combine these two if they feel less than the woman. If a woman is wealthier than her date, a pathetic men will say make that a focus. Does it matter if a woman makes more money? Who makes more money, the prostitute or the pimp? See? It is about frame of control and not who grinds for the cash. Ignore the elements that make you feel less than and heighten the elements that make you feel confident. There are many sad men who will bring up their insecurities on dates because they feel that pity will somehow work in their favor. Listen closely. *Women will never pity men.* Read that again. And so do not seek pity with women. It is anti-seductive and a massive waste of time. A man can be a working-class carpenter but still his pride can be stronger than a woman who is a lawyer. It is about the frame of thought we set for women to think inside. It is not about the reality itself but how we let reality affect us. And woman are mojo leaches. They feed on the energy and pride the man is showcasing. This is why men should avoid all speech that is self-deprecating or pity seeking.

Giving false choices is a way to manipulate a conversation into the frame we want. For example, if a man wants a woman to come back to his house, he could say "Want to come over?" Or he could say "Let's meet up. My place or yours" – See? The first example allows the woman think about the offered choice and her own choice in opposition. But the second example narrows the woman into a mental corner by offering a "complete" set of choices that both lead to private meeting. Instead of the woman thinking of rejection, she will be confining herself to the choices offered. This can help a man when he is setting up dates. If a man says "I'm free Friday. Want to meet up?" then this allows the woman to reject him by saying "I'm busy Friday. What are you doing on...?" Which may be true but still it is a shit test to date planning. The woman is displaying that she is busier than the man while leading the man in setting up the date time. Or the woman will reject the man outright without giving her own direction "Cannot do Friday" It is better for the man to say "Let's meet up. I am free Friday or next Monday. Either work for you?" This narrows the woman's mind to pick one or the other. Instead of her thinking of rejecting the man, she is thinking about whether she is free on either day. It leads her thought from the only two choices provided. It is not just about whether the woman wants to meet up but rather which day she is free to meet up. See? A manipulate effect to focus her mind. This is what leaders do. We must lead minds. And this requires us to play 3D chess to a degree in our language. It is not about the first move; it is about leading a strategy many moves ahead.

Another point to discuss on language is certainty of self. A man must remove "I think..."

"Kind of..." "Uh..." and "Maybe" from his language. He must speak with certainty to inspire confidence. If a man is stumbling through his language with doubt, then why would a woman every trust his speech? It is crucial for a man to focus his mind on the many doubt-filled words he is peppering his speech with. Do not use qualifiers in speech but rather just speak. If someone wants to challenge then let them. Do not needlessly challenge yourself to avoid confrontation. This is a coward's path and unframed. Be proud and certain. This sets the frame of thought for the woman and allows her to trust you enough for submission.

Another point is avoiding awkward silences. This is especially crucial in the beginning stages of dating. It shows the man is not imaginative enough to lead a conversation. It is failure of leadership and anti-seductive. But this does not mean that a man should avoid letting a healthy pause happen to inspire the woman's anxious speaking. When a man holds back from responding for a few seconds after a woman speaks will many times encourage her to continue speaking which sets the frame of her being in qualification mode. Most women will trail off after answering a question and then if there is a pregnant pause; the woman will fill the empty air with added speech. This is because women are socially anxious creatures that want to both expand their expression while being of service to the need of the situation by preventing awkward silence. Allow *pregnant pauses* but do not let the conversation die. If there is no speaking for more than ten seconds with no food or experience will incite massive anxiety in the woman. She will want to run to the exit because of the uncomfortable chemistry. If a man is leading a conversation correctly, he will avoid these energy drains.

Another point to consider is how the man narrates his feelings about the experience. For example, at the end of the date if a man is the first to say "I had a good time tonight" is cornball language that removes the mystery of his thoughts. It is best to end the date with a level of mystery that inflates the woman's imagination. For example, a man can signal the date is ending by putting on his coat or paying for the bar tab. Then he can walk the woman to her car and say "I'll text you sometime. Bye" - See? What meaning can be interpreted in this? It is calm and certain with mystery. The man is the one who has the power to reengage with the woman he so chooses. If a man wants to set up another date at the end of a first date can be a positive but is dependent on chemistry

Beyond

the

burden

The greatest attractant for women is a man being beyond the burden of reality. It is supreme greed that exists in a woman's heart. And this is why women are more animalistic than men which allows them to be gamed. A man must be beyond the challenges of life because a woman is burdened by her biology. She is overwhelmed by the chaos of life. This is why women tend to over indulge and get fat. They need relief to the pressures of life. They need relief from the challenges of existence. Inside their mind is the programming that they will soon be overburdened with the expansion of child in womb. Their body will become loaded down in the ending months of pregnancy which means they will need a provider/protector to that need. Women crave men who are beyond the burden of reality because they crave a man to make their life easier. A man must represent being "Beyond the burden" of existence to draw women into his orbit. This is why a ladies' man is seen as "Cool" and "Smooth" It is the spirit of abundance that makes a man transcend the desperate worry of the masses who showcase their burdened states. Women are more sexual than men. They see sex everywhere they look. But instead of the just sexualizing the body like a man, a woman will sexualize the world that surrounds a man. How well-groomed is the man? Does he have a nice haircut and does he groom his facial hair? SEX. What kind of clothes does the man wear? Are they expensive or cheap? SEX. How tall is the man and is he strong looking? SEX. Does the man drive a small dependable car, an expensive car or a big truck? SEX. What kind of job does the man have? Does he make more money? SEX. Is the man popular and does he get attention from other women? SEX. How does a man handle shit tests, with calm charisma or emotional reaction? SEX.

Note these. Because at the heart of all these are that a man is beyond the burden that most are overwhelmed by. A woman wants walking success so she can associate herself to it. A woman wants a man who is not affected by the chaos of reality. While a man will sexualize a woman's body, a woman will sexualize everything that surrounds a man's life. If a man drives up to a date with a beat up, small car with a cracked windshield is ANTI-SEXUAL. If a man needs a haircut and is not groomed properly is ANTI-SEXUAL. If a man is wearing cheap clothes that are dirty is ANTI-SEXUAL. If a man is poor and struggles financially is ANTI-SEXUAL. If a man is short and weak looking is ANTI-SEXUAL.

The core thing to remember is that if a man looks burdened by existence, he will repel women. Why would a woman want to join a man's world if he is burdened by it? Think. A man must master his own reality in order for it to look appealing to the greed in a woman's heart. This is why women will fight over a few men. It is a few men that ascend reality and then live a life of abundance. This is the Matthew Principle. In Mark 4:25 it says "For whoever has, to him more will be given; and whoever does not have, even what he has will be taken away from him." Abundance breeds abundance. Women give to those that do not need. Women reward those that already have. "Already have" is a transcendence of desperation. And desperation is how a man pushes a woman away. He must be beyond his own desires in order to receive. A man who hides his thirst will soon be in a flood of reward. This is the mindset that attracts women. "Cool" means to be above what drags others down. "Smooth" means to not be affected by what others react to. A man who shows up to a date well groomed, dressed nicely and driving a nice car/truck is already flooding a woman with sexual desire. He reaffirms that he is beyond the burden by assuming leadership, avoiding awkward silences and deflecting shit tests. And then he showcases that he is beyond the need of the woman's company by cutting the date short. *The man who needs nothing and will receive everything.* This is the key to understanding women. They complain about the unfairness of reality while rewarding those who already have abundance. Women will trip and fall over each other in order to reward a man who has zero need. But there is an innate reason women want to be with a man who is beyond the burden. A woman craves masculine authority because a woman craves to be under a strong frame. The frame is a shelter against the anxiety of existence. Whomever is the dominant in the relationship is the one exposed to the harshness of reality. The submissive can be more irresponsible while the dominant shields from chaos of life. A woman who seeks a man who is beyond the burden is like a someone who is seeking shelter in a storm. She wants to go under the frame that is beyond the burden. Women look around at men and say "Can he shield me from the burden of life?" --- When a woman goes on a date with an ungroomed man who drives a shitty car, wears cheap clothes and becomes emotional during shit tests is like someone fleeing a storm only to run under an umbrella covered in holes. The man himself cannot shield the woman from the burden of reality and so she will sexually reject him.

Women innately know they have this primitive greed that is selfish. But how do they protect themselves from feeling animalistic in desire? Emotion. A woman will emotionally attach herself to a man who is beyond the burden and this emotionalism will make her feel that she is beyond her own animal greed. In a way, a woman gaslights herself into believing in love to spare herself her own brutality. But remember, a woman will not emotionally attach herself to something that cannot fulfill her greed. The greed must be satisfied first and then the emotions will make her forget that it was the initial greed that made her attach herself to the man. And this emotionalism will make a woman feel righteous in her decision because women moralize emotion. A woman will use her head to decipher all the key ingredients to her passion and then when they are fulfilled; then she will open her heart for love. It is a revision of reality that allows a woman to feel that she is not greedy or brutal in her own view of existence. Women only date up. They look for men who are better in key ways that fall into leader/protector/provider. Sound romantic? Of course, it is not. Sexual selection is not romantic. That is why women will paint over the reality of sexual selection with emotionalism but only after their primitive needs are met. It is up to a man to make sure these needs are met in a woman for her to grow in emotion. And it is the emotion that secures the pair bond. Once that emotion is spiked, the power balance shifts to the man's favor.

Stumbling

steps

scares

the

birds

In previous chapters we discussed the importance of a man leading a conversation. But a common mistake men make when leading a conversation is when they turn it into an oppressive interview. They ask a question and then after the woman answers they ask another question. This repeats over and over which kills the sexual chemistry. It is socially awkward behavior. A conversation that is intriguing and stimulating is one that is not robotic. And it takes little charisma to merely ask questions. This does not mean that questions are incorrect but rather that the man who asks a question should give a little of his own thoughts after the woman's answer before digging deeper into the discussion with another question. Many awkward men will ask a question and then after the woman answers they will feel lost. And what will they do? They will either ask a question that furthers their last question or they will even more awkwardly shift the conversation by ignoring the answer altogether by asking a new topical question. The world is full of low charisma guys who think being the interviewer on a date is leading the conversation. It is a low thinking tactic for leadership. A good approach to communicating with a woman is to ask a question and then to give a thoughtful reply on her answer before digging deeper with another question. Men who fail to sprinkle their own views/ideas into the mixture are uncharismatic. It is like a wooden step that clumsily scares off the women. To be smooth means to help a woman navigate the communication by listening to her and adding thoughtful commentary. Question after question after question is inexperienced and drains sexual chemistry. And many questions are mundane which incite little to no imagination.

What kind of question should a man ask a woman? The questions that lift her ego. But not directly. It must be subtle. For example, "What inspires you in life?" – This question allows a personal and egocentric response. It is a challenging question that creates a healthy qualifying anxiety to form. The more questions that provoke a woman into thought while allowing her to focus on her own ego is seductive. Women are not seduced by men; they are seduced by themselves. It is a woman's mind that creates romance, not the man. The man is simply a guide for the woman to navigate her own arousal. It is the woman's ego and her imagination that leads her to romantic passions. Think about how to get a woman to talk about herself. Not talking about her looks but rather everything but her looks. See? This is unexpected because a man's sexual selection is not based on a woman's mind but rather her body. Women know this deeply and so when a man focuses on everything but a woman's body in conversation is seen as intriguing. "Who is this mysterious man?" the woman will think. Why? Because it is a mystery to a woman why a man would be interested in her beyond what is physical. It is a tactic to build initial interest. Is the man genuinely interested in the mind over the body? No. We are men, our sexuality is based on a woman's body. But by overcoming this primitive algorithm we can bypass a woman's defenses. Asking sincere questions on a woman's thoughts, hopes and life all increase sexual arousal because the elephant in the room is being ignored. This ignoring of the obvious sexual desire will inflame curiosity and passion. When a man hides his sexual intent is seductive. But this does not mean hiding the intent altogether. For example, while a man is avoiding sexual speech, he will be touching a woman in "non sexual" ways like hand touching/arm touching which makes a woman think about sex because it is non obvious. What is not obvious incites fantasy and imagination. This is why a man who leads a woman on fun non sexual topics spikes the sexual thoughts in her head. What we hide is what will be thought about. This is seductive and charismatic. The key to seductive behavior is to make a woman think about sex without being obvious about making her think about sex. And this comes from playing it cool and relaxed. Think about how many sexually thirsty guys a woman has to deal with in romance. Most guys cannot control their thirst which causes them to talk about a woman's beauty and to sexualize the conversation too early in the beginning stages. This approach reeks of mundane desperations. Hide what you most want. Conceal the beating and primitive desire. *What is hidden is most thought about.* Women are attracted to mystery and a man who hides his sexual intent is fueling his own mystery. Do not be dull in conversation by beating a woman over the head with obsessive questioning. And do not overly sexualize the conversation too early in the relationship Be engaged, listen and lead the woman to her own desires.

We

hide

weakness

As men we know that women ask for vulnerability and yet punish weakness. Women will punish weakness until the end. And no time period is more volatile in attraction than the early stages of sexual selection. In my book The Wall Speaks, I wrote about how a man can carry a strong and proud frame. This is power projection that builds power within and projects power without. It showcases power which is the greatest aphrodisiac to women. Women reward strength and punish weakness. And a woman cannot afford to pity a man whom she must depend on for a protector/provider role once she becomes incapacitated with child in womb. This is a key point for a man to understand in dating. A woman is incapable of pitying a man because she has too much emotional anxiety. This anxious state makes her pity herself above a man whom she is seeking to lead her in strength. Remember, a woman is drawn to a man who is beyond the burden of existence. This is why it is key that a man project confidence in his own reality and hide his personal weaknesses. What could be a weakness that a man would need to hide? It could be anything. But for example, a man may have little to no friends. If a woman picks up that a man is anti-social will kill her attraction. Why? Because being a loner is extra challenging in existence and requires extra intellectual strength. And most men do not have this extra strength which means them being loners is seen as a negative. This state will be seen as burdensome to women. How can a man succeed in sexual selection when he has weakness in some areas? Do not admit the weakness. Direct all attention and conversation away from it. In the beginning stages of romance, it will be about the man and woman alone. The connection is built on pairing off on adventures. And this does not require friends or partying in most scenarios. During this time period, a man should be showing his strength of authority through framed leadership while hiding the elements that would kill the initial chemistry. The more a woman sniffs out weakness in the beginning the more apt she will be to sexually reject the man in favor of a man who is more complete in the necessities of her sexual needs.

Many men on first dates will think that pity will have a positive effect on building a connection. Why would they think such a foolish thought? It is because they were groomed to believe in "Just be yourself" They think, we can bond over our shared weaknesses. Wouldn't that be wonderful? It is an illusion. A woman does not want to bond over weakness. She wants to bond herself to strength above her. And this requires a man to be beyond the burden of existence. This is what it means to be "Cool" and confident. Feminized men will think "Let's talk about our doubts, fears and anxieties. Through discussing the darkness within we will bond closer in friendship" – What these fools do not realize is that a woman is scanning for all weakness for a romantic partner. She does not want a friend; she wants a leader. And once we see the weakness of our leaders, we replace them. This is the reality of being alive. Women do not want friends who share weakness, they crave leaders who showcase strength. A man must be aware of his own weaknesses that are anti seductive and hide them. Until when? It depends on the weakness but many weaknesses can be hidden until a strong emotional attachment forms. Once a woman attaches herself emotionally to a man, she will be more willing to overlook his weaknesses. In fact, she will defend his weakness as strength the more she is emotionally attached. This is why a man should only focus on building the emotional attachment before letting a woman see behind the curtain of his reality. Emotional attachment is the trap that secures pair bonding in our species. Love makes us blind to the imperfections of others. And this is crucial for many men who are struggling in their own lives. Too many men think they must be honest about their weaknesses up front. This is not how romance or sexual selection works. How do we cook a frog? We place it in warm water and slowly turn up the heat. This is the same for gaming women. We project that we are beyond the burden which acclimates a woman to our world. And by the time the imperfections are revealed; the waters of passions are already hot. Emotional entrapment is game. Women also hide their weaknesses. Both sides hide what may scare the other aware. Women tell men to "Just be themselves" because they want to reject bad romance before emotional attachment forms. It helps them and hurts men. As men we have tremendous challenge in sexual selection and we need all the help we can get. This is why I write. And a man must understand the importance of "Frame of thought" We construct the frame of thinking for others to think inside. If a man is proud of his existence, a woman will share that thought. This requires a man to not just be truthful with his inner chaos but to establish order that transcends his own inner state. Construct the frame that projects that you are beyond the burden of existence and watch as women flock to that frame. Women want to escape the burden of their own existence. They want to join a world that is not suffering. And if a man projects that he is struggling in life during the initial phases of romance; why in the hell would a woman want to join him? See? Do not forget that a man who bluffs in poker can not only win one hand but the entire game. *The truth of a man is whatever helps him to succeed.* Why would anxiety, doubt and fear represent a man's truth of self? That is a perceptional issue. Whatever hides our fear is truth. Whatever helps us overcome our doubt and anxieties is truth. Our perception is truth, not just the bare bones reality. *Dreams are truth.* And when we showcase strength to secure emotional attachment before revealing weakness is truth. It is the truth of sexual selection. Do not believe the lies.

We

hide

truth

in

the

beginning

     Women by nature are more agreeable and have a greater trait openness than men. And now more than ever women are non-religious which means they are detached from traditionalism. When a woman is living alone for long periods of time, she will reaffirm these innate qualities into her outlook on reality. It is feminine consciousness unbounded. In our times we see traditionalism fading fast into a new borderless mania. And what does agreeableness with openness mean in regard to a woman's worldview? It means that women by in large will be more collectivist and sexually liberated in their views of reality. Their high empathic emotionalism and social cowardice drives them to ideology that is oppressive to individualism. Their ideology will be "Be accepting of all sexualities and giving to all in meritless collectivism" The more single women that accumulate with the chaos of current sexual selection in western civilization means that feminine consciousness is growing unbounded. It is growing without a check from masculine consciousness. Women are becoming pure political animals without any anchoring of children or religion. This means that with every year sexual acceptance is expanding into darker territories because no clear boundary is being established. There are no rules to feminine consciousness which means that it snowballs into madness. Their trait openness is accelerating to a point where children will soon be damaged by the high indoctrination of this all accepting sexuality. And women will increase Marxist ideology because the spirit of merit-based competition is overwhelming to women without male providers. Women who must depend on themselves into old age is a nightmare to their existence. Feminists who were told to be career women will forsake it as they despair and grow tired from age. Career women in capitalism will flip to bureaucrats of a new socialist order. Remember it is much easier to say "I believe in give a man a fish" politic publicly than the more disciplined and individualistic "Teach a man a fish" politic of self-reliance. A woman's overreliance on groups for emotional regulation leads them to mass conformity. And this will accelerate a woman's feminine politic in our societies, a symptom of hyperfeminization. Men and women are not just becoming more separate in person but in fundamental belief. *The sexes are spiraling into chaos as they are being torn apart from each other.* Now more than ever men are failing in sexual selection as they retreat to virtual fantasy. After more than half a century after the sexual revolution, we have more virgin men than ever before while children are being sexually groomed by feminists into non reproductive behaviors. Many men are losing hope in civilization because men have forgotten their own power. A forgotten generation of fatherless men have been told to submit to their female peers. They have been given video game controllers while their female peers are given the keys to the kingdom. What can a man do during this period of mass chaos? What can a man do when he goes out on dates with women who are ideologically opposed to him on a fundamental level? Do not give up hope. We are biological creatures that are designed for sexual selection. The times might be changing but our primitive algorithms have not changed. A woman is imprisoned by her biological conditioning into mass conformity from her feminine consciousness. This is why it is easy to game women. Individuals are hard to discern but collectivists easily give themselves away.

A woman can be gamed and a woman can be framed. Remember, a woman will feel herself to be special by superficial means. She will dye her hair, cover herself in tattoos and preach deviant sexualities but behind the act is a human female that is susceptible to sexual selection like all human females. Ideology does not control women, emotion does. And a man who can control a woman's emotions will be able to control her ideologies. A woman's emotionalism allows her to attach herself to a man. And what does that mean? Women who fall for men lose themselves. *To be IN love is to lose sense of identity.* This is why when a woman gets strong emotional attachment to a man, she will imitate his tastes and philosophies. A man who is inexperienced with women will think that he found a special woman who likes all the things he likes. The woman likes the man and that is why she likes the things he likes. All women do this to a degree with the men they are with. And the greater the man's frame the more the woman will attune herself to his frame of thinking. This is the code behind the charade of identity that a woman parades in her own "Individualism" A woman was not designed to be strong and independent. She was designed to be vulnerable and dependent. This biological programming allows our species to connect and propagate. And this is why a man should not lose hope in the great divide of the sexes during the chaos of our hyperfeminized times. Women might be a world away in their thinking but they can be brought close through emotional attachment. *Love will save the world.* But let us define love since most use the word with feeling but without articulation. Love means to lose sense of self in bliss. It is self-sacrifice and a forgetting of self. To be IN love is to sacrifice self to the other. A woman who falls in love with a man will make great sacrifices to keep the attachment. This is the power shift in romance that allows a check to the overwhelming feminine consciousness that spikes outside masculine frame. We will solve the vast divide of separation between men and women with love.

The first few dates a man goes on with a woman will have low emotional attachment. This is why a man should omit fundamental differences between feminine/masculine ideology during the beginning stages of sexual selection. Once emotional attachment is had in romance is when a woman can align herself with the man's frame. But not before. This is why political discussions and discussions on gender fluidity should be omitted from the initial stages of dating. Remember, a woman is far in separation to masculine consciousness and must be persuaded through emotion to abandon her views. And this will close the gap between the fundamental differences that are exploding in our times. It is easy for a woman to reject and dismiss a man she has zero emotional investment in. This is why guys who bring up controversial topics on the first date are just giving the woman a reason to reject them. A first date is not the time for power shifting and freedom of ideological expression. First emotion must rise then attachment forms which creates the loss of self-needed for power transfer. Do not skip these steps. As men we incite emotional attachment in women which causes them to lose themselves enough for pair bonding. This is how a "Strong, independent woman" will fall into feminine submission in a relationship. The emotionalism inside a woman is how they align themselves as compliments to men with strong frames. Men with weak frames do not inspire this "Loss of self" that is needed for harmony between the sexes. A man must be framed and dominant which allows the woman to be unframed and submissive. This polarity between men and women fuels success in our sexual selection.

Shattering

the

fear

Many men have drowned in water not because they did not know how to swim but because the overwhelming variables of water flooded their thinking and made them lose their senses to hysteria. This can be like life. Calm heads prevail. It is the calmness of mind that allows us to transcend the chaos of storms. When we calm ourselves, we project wealth of confidence that attracts others trust. And our calm nerves help us to navigate challenging situations which require focus. It takes calm nerves and mastery of breath to penetrate a bullseye with an arrow. The same for a romance.

Fear is broken into two. High nerves that shake the water out of our glass. And frozen fear that prevents us from picking up the glass. Two key differences to fear. One may lead to the other. Remember the brilliant words from Frank Herbert "Fear is the mind killer" – It is the fear inside us that shakes away our potential in waste or freezes us within ourselves. Both are self-harming to a man's potential opportunities in life and both harm a man in sexual selection. We either ruin opportunities with shaky nerves or we miss opportunities because the fear freezes our action. If a man is able to play beautiful music alone but plays bad music because his nerves get the best of him in public; how can others see what he has to offer? If a man has brilliant thoughts but they trip and stumble over his tongue; how can others know him? If a man holds tight to himself because he is afraid of stumbling before others; what life is he living? Do you see? It is not good enough to simply be, we must master our presentation of self to let others know what we truly are. This is the same with a man who is going on a date. If he shows nervous energy with a woman will only increase her nervous anxiety and increase her doubt about him. Women are empaths and feed on energy. When a man shows calm charisma with a woman allows the woman to align herself with that energy. It draws her in and keeps her in orbit. Many guys ask how to approach women. This has less to do with rationale and more to do with their fear. They are overthinking it which makes them nervous. How does a man approach a woman? He approaches her. That does not require an entire chapter in a book to write about. A man who fears water will not swim. But a man who jumps into water will soon learn to swim and overcome his fears. This is the same with sexual selection. Do not fear mistakes or rejection. It is an experience and beginning experiences are usually awkward. But they teach us valuable lessons for future opportunities. And desensitization therapy is key to overcoming the dual fears of nervous breakdown/frozen action. We must acclimate ourselves to what we fear and we must summon the will to face the fear. It is the fear that ruins most romance. And desperation itself is a symptom of fear. When a man acts desperate with a woman will flood her with fear. She will be consumed by the man's weakness which will repel her. How can a man overcome his shaky nerves? He must realize that it is all in the mind. We control our perception and that perception alters our consciousness. Once our mind obeys then our breath obeys. A man has more control over his mind and body than he realizes. Sometimes it takes a lifetime to figure this out. But better late than never. One way a man can conquer fear is to realize how anxious women innately are. For example, when a man is going on a date and has anxiety; he can remind himself "She is just as nervous as me, if not more so" And this is the truth. Also, the calmer a man makes himself the more the woman will be reminded of her own nerves. Knowing someone else is struggling with their sense of self is fuel for reaffirming ourself. This is the same in combat, war, business negotiation and romance. When we see the opposing side show nerves emboldens us in strength. We feed on fear. How can a man flip the fear from himself to the woman in a romantic way? Assuming a role is how a man can transcend himself. Just like soldiers, firemen and policemen overcome themselves in acts of duty, the same can be done in romance. Become a masculine leader and realize that it is not just for stimulating the woman sexually but that she is emotionally needing a man who fulfills that role. There are singers who get nervous when publicly speaking or talking in interviews. These types will become calm when performing music because they are thinking of the role itself and less about themselves outside that role. When we focus our thoughts on a duty to perform is how we overcome our nerves. And that lowering of the man's nerves will make the woman herself become more self-consciousness. *A calm man creates a nervous woman.* But the nervous woman will attract herself to the man to feed on his calm energy. This is what we call "Good chemistry" The man is showing no fear which creates anxiety in the woman (From self-consciousness) which leads her to enter his frame to calm herself. And how long does it take this energy shift from woman to man? How long does it take a woman to give her energy to the man and to fall into qualification mode from being made anxious from her self-consciousness? Seconds. Minutes. This is all. But most guys reveal their nerves in the first five minutes of an approach/date with a woman that shifts power immediately to her side since she becomes emboldened. And then the chemistry dies. A woman knows whether or not she wants to have sex with a man within the first five minutes of interaction. It does not take long for a woman to understand a man's energy and authority of self. And authority of self is the key thing to remember. If the power shift happens in seconds/minutes is like holding the breath in water. Back when I was a kid, I would play swimming pool games with my friends. Who could hold their breath the longest under the water? Whomever breaks surface first loses. Holding the breath takes concentration and authority of self. How we breathe is how we think. Breathing is a mental action that requires mental focus. When a man can manage his nerves for just a few minutes in the initial interaction with a woman will incite her nerves which will embolden the man to further increase his authority over her. Then she will fall into a follower role from that beginning phase which fuels her arousal. And all it took was a man to master his nerves for a few moments to power shift. When we are thrown into chaos it is the order that keeps us not only afloat but allows us to swim through it. This is why it is crucial for man to learn frame when he is interacting with a woman. Masculine order allows a man to overcome feminine chaos. The more framed a man presents himself the more submissive the woman will be with him. It is the fundamental understanding of polarity between the sexes. Men who believe in equality in romance are ignorant of polarity. They do not realize that masculine leadership creates feminine submission. And that a man's submission will create feminine leadership. It is either one or the other. When a man fulfils his role as masculine leader will increase his success in sexual selection because it is the polarity that women seek. They seek leaders so that they can receive the pleasure of being in feminine submission. Women who are dominant with men kill their sex drives and end up cucking the men they are paired with. It is against the natural selection of our species for women to be dominant over men. It creates chaos, dysfunction, unhappiness and ruins romance. Seek leadership. Overcome the nerves that rattle the cage of being. Project a strong sense of self and then watch as women reward it.

Leave

shadows

in

your

wake

Women love using their feminine intuition. They love mystery because it allows them to pine. And pining is the heart of romance. "Absence makes the heart fonder" - But before absence there must be excitement. A woman must pine for the last emotional memory of an experience. It is crucial that a man not be overly available to a woman so that he builds mystery with her. Remember, leaders are busy and distant. And women crave leaders. The more a man understands romance the more he will understand it is about spiking emotion and then leaving a mystery behind. How can a man do this? It can be through exciting a woman through messaging and then "dragging her" To drag means to purposely avoid/ignore her for a period of time. Dragging a woman is what keeps her invested within the fantasy of her mind. A woman does not fall in love with a man narrating his passion but by the man allowing her to narrate her own fantasy. *The less a man speaks the more a woman must think*. See? What do we hear women say when they are complaining about men that they are in a relationship with? "I wish my man would open up. I wish he would communicate more" – These women are chasing these men's affections and the mystery drives them up the wall. It creates a deep feeling of indignation mixed with arousal. Remember, a woman is a dual creature and her arousal is dual in nature. A woman will complain about being happy and then be unhappy when there is nothing to complain about. This is why female complaint should be understood with a higher understanding of female nature. Women complain the most about the men they are most invested with. And a woman is most happy when her man supplies her the mixture of indignation/mystery/excitement. Do "Nice guys" supply women with these key elements? No. They fear creating indignation, leave no mystery and bore women with their agreeableness.

How can a man get a woman to think about him? He must be different from other men. This can be done through multiple paths. A man can lead a woman on an action date, lead her in brief conversations that sprinkles a little of his interesting mind/life. And then end with bold physical advancement. The bold physical advancement will make a woman invest herself if she allows it past her defenses. Then the man can distance himself to the woman's bodily investment which will fuel her doubt and will have her spinning her emotional wheels over him. And when he returns all the irritation/indignation will dissolve with his reintroduced validation. A spike in connection. Excite and leave. See?

Another way a man can do this is through another path. He should have sexual restraint which confuses the woman and increases mystery. But first he must incite sexual arousal with subtle touching/kissing. Lead a woman on "Sweet dates" which could be as simple as walking through a park. He would lead her by the hand and lead her in conversation. The dates are short and sweet. Then he could plan a date at the end that gives her enough time for days to think about him without communication. This allows her to pine for him while waiting for his return. A few sweet dates that build attraction and mystery. What is the mystery? It is the man holding back his sexual energy and leaving the woman with a feeling. That is the key. Why would holding back sexual boldness incite mystery? Because most men are sexually thirty and most women are overwhelmed by sexual opportunity. When an attractive man hides his sexual intent spikes the mystery on when and whether he will make his move. To hide sexual intent is to fuel mystery. It displays measurement, control and discipline which are all masculine elements. What a woman is most flooded with by the majority of men is withheld by one man. See? Then leave her thinking. Leave the woman with a feeling like a jewel that she can hold in her hands. A jewel of passion that she can gaze at in the man's absence. She will pine for him and her emotional attachment will build.

Either path leads to success in emotional attachment and success in sexual selection. In both cases a man should not be messaging/calling the woman between dates and if so; done rarely. Many men kill their mystery and kill the distance that builds attraction by messaging the woman the next day with a lame "Good morning beautiful" or some pathetic message. Or they will drain a woman of not only mystery but emotional energy by messaging the woman the next day after a date with "What are you up to?" What the hell does that man think she is up to? She is living life and now she must expend energy in a mundane response. It is best to drag a woman after a date for a while and then drop a message that is setting up a future meet up. Nothing kills sexual energy more than draining a woman of her emotional energy. And this mundane messaging kills romantic potential.

The rhythm of romance is like fishing. Remember, a woman can be gamed because she has common patterns for exploitation and has greed that drives her forward. Fishing has long been tied to dating because of multiple reasons. A man must master his techniques to catch fish and different fish requires different techniques. He must not only understand the fish but himself in the process. Above and below. There are a few sayings that men tell each other in sexual selection, one is "There are plenty of fish in the sea" when rejected/failed romance happens. This saying helps men to emotionally detach from their failure to focus on future opportunities. Another is "If you are fishing, would you take advice from the fisherman or the fish?" This means that the object of the hunt (Woman) would lead astray and better to get advice from men who must use their imagination and technique in the hunt.

Now going back to the discussion at hand and its application to fishing. A man sets bait on his fishhook and adds a lure. Then he may let it sit for the fish to notice. But then he will reel/tug his line to imitate live bait. This movement is excitement to the fish and the fish will pursue. It is this presentation of desire with tug and pull that is similar to romance. A man will present himself as an attractive masculine leader and then will tug that lure away from the woman. The woman will then pursue him inside her mind.

She will invest herself in the greed of her own heart. To drag a woman is to lead her to the core of her desire. Present and pull. Present and pull. *Present and pull.* See? This is a sexual rhythm that at the very base of our nature is like sex. The erection penetrates and pulls out. And that repetition proceeds until climax. It is the same for physical interactions in the early stages of sexual selection. A presentation of desire and a removal of that lure. Then a reintroduction of that desire but this time heightened in sensitivity and a removal once again. In and out. In and out. *In and out.* Think about what fun means to a woman. It means a man who is "Beyond the burden" of reality making splashy appearances into a woman's life and then disappearing just as dramatically as his entrance. This is a reason that a man should make dates relatively short and exciting. Then proceed to drag the woman emotionally through distance for a period before making an appearance with another meet up. And this process can repeat as the woman builds in emotional attachment with arousal. If a woman agrees to give her number to a man, if a woman agrees to go out on a date with a man, if a woman agrees to go home with a man is on the man to screw up. Remember that. If there is a romantic failure during any of those levels requires contemplation on what went wrong. It is always the man's fault. *To be a man is to bear the responsibility of all things.* Do not let the failure consume but always pull a learning lesson from it. Then alter strategy for another attempt with another woman. This is romance. This is the sexual selection of our species. We bait women with the heart of their desires and we pull away to incite mystery and to draw their attention to us. Stop flooding a woman with validation and mundane messages that zap her of emotional energy and yourself of mystery. Place the bait and then slowly pull it to shore.

Desperate

hunters

risk

parasites

A hungry hunter who fails to catch big game will resort to smaller game. And many different kinds of small game contain parasites. This is the same for dating but replace parasites with sexually transmitted disease and unethical behaviorism. Or it could be that a man lowers his standards to women that would hurt his pride/esteem. Many men will fall into these different scenarios from sexual thirst/loneliness/low self-esteem. This falls into the category of vetting a woman. What is a good woman compared to a bad woman in sexual selection? A whore may be easy to have sex with but at what risk of disease? And a whore may be easy but the easiness itself can hurt a man's pride as what is easy for him may be easy for others. It goes beyond disease alone and to the ego. Another thing is when a woman is unethical/insane that leads to harvesting a devil in the fishing net of passion. When we accept bad influences in our life, they can plague us like hidden demons who haunt. Never hunt crazy. That is a haunting a man does not want have. Remember, feminine is chaos and most women deserve to be forgotten and wise men want to be forgotten by these women. What does it mean to have sex with a land whale of a woman? And I am not talking about a curvy woman who is a little chubby. There are some big mommas out there and desperate men will surrender their pride to them. And this pride surrender will hurt a man when he is seeking a woman who is not beautiful enough for his own desires. But let us focus on STDs. The more a woman sleeps with different men the more apt she will be to having disease. How can a man tell if a woman has had many previous partners in sex? How does she dress? If a woman is dressing scantily, she is used to selling her sexual appeal. This means that she is a proud seller and has had previous buyers. Look for more modest dressed women. How much makeup and jewelry does she wear? A woman who is painted up like a prostitute, with giant hoop earrings, long nails and high heels will be used to advertising for sex. Avoid. How many tattoos, piercings? How old is she? Tattoos and piercings tend to fall into impulsive/physical harm. And what is impulsive/physical harm as well? *Sleeping around.* That is why women with lots of tattoos and piercings tend to have high sexual experience. If a woman falls into this category and is older than she will have more experience in sex than a younger woman who falls into this category. A woman who professes her loyalty is most likely disloyal. Why? Because women use speech as affirmations. They speak in hope after failure in behavior. When a woman says that she is loyal, what she is saying is she is *reassuring herself of her hope for her own loyalty.* And nothing is more useless than hopeful words. What is her history? And regardless of history, a woman is loyal to frame and disloyal to weakness. How can a woman know she will be loyal to a man? She does not. She will become disloyal to a man dependent on the man's current frame. Men who let their frames get weak inspire sexual heat in their women for other men.

Another thing a man should look out for with a woman is whether or not she had a respected father or an absent father. Why? Because this will let a man know how a woman has been conditioned to view his own authority. If she has been conditioned to view male authority as a positive will make her easier to frame. Also, a woman's sexuality will become more chaotic the weaker or more absent her father was in her life. Why? If a woman had a weak/absent father she will have had no strong protection of her sexual expression. But there is a deeper reason to be careful with these types of women. Emasculated males create sexual heat in their women which causes women to cuck them. A woman who was raised by a weak father will have seen her mother in constant sexual heat for other men. This will have conditioned her to be in sexual heat herself. And years of sexual conditioning will be difficult to frame. She will view disloyalty as natural to existence because it is all she has been taught by example. She will have seen her mother disrespecting her father and flirting with other men. This was her father's fault for shrugging frame and for being weak. To be a man is to bear the responsibility of all things. But a man's daughter will be a product of his own frame. And emasculated fathers will have conditioned their daughters for sexual heat and unstable sexual behaviors. Be careful with women who do not respect their fathers and whose mother does not respect her husband. It is previous programming in sexual selection.

Another thing a man should think about is a woman's mental health. This is a sensitive topic since single women will have more issues with mental stability from the fact that they are outside strong masculine frames to lower their innate neuroticism. Does a woman have a father and what is her relationship to him? Women without fathers have more sexual chaos (More sexualized and less loyal) And they will be more challenging to frame. It does not mean that all fatherless women are like this but a man should expect this to a degree. How many friends does a woman have and what is her relationship with her family? The more alienated a woman is from her roots the more unstable she will be in her mind. Women depend on social networks more than men which means that loner women are more mentally unwell than loner men. Does she drink and smoke a lot? Does she hang out in clubs and bars? These women will have more sexual experience and will be conditioned to be less loyal in relationships. How much does a woman shit test a man on the first date/approach? The more testing up front, the more testing there will be later in relationship. Chemistry should be relatively stable/easy in early stages of sexual selection. If there is drama on the first few dates is a harbinger of things to come. How much sarcasm does she use? This is passive aggressive testing and disrespect. The more sarcastic a woman the weaker the men in her life. Does she like babies/children? Look for nurturing and empathy as key elements in finding a quality woman. Does she read books and what kind? Does she like dark media/horror/occult? This could imply that she gets excited by non-societal norms which could affect her sexuality. Does she protect her sexuality in the first few dates? *A woman who is easy to get will be easy to lose.* Women who have been trained to view their sexuality as sacred will carry that into a relationship which protects the pair bond. Is she asking for money/favors early in the dating period? She is looking to exploit. Does she have children and how many? She is wanting a protector/provider for another man's children and wanting a man to save her from her own bad decisions. This is especially true when a woman has many children all by different fathers. A major warning of sexual chaos. We have a world of single mothers with kids needing framed leadership. Do not overly demonize single mothers like immature guys. If a woman is truly worth a relationship, then raising an orphan can be a positive in some situations. But do not feel that you must be a savior to these women or children. Figure out the best deal for yourself.

Listen to how a woman talks about her exes. Does she demonize them all? Did she say that her previous men were abusive narcissists? This could tell more about the woman herself than the men she is talking about. Women will refuse to take accountability by nature and will place blame on men when relationships fail. This is to be expected. Does she still communicate with her previous men? Does she have male friends (And especially gay male friends) A woman should have limited association with all men except her current man. If a woman is in communication with her exes, then old passions can easily return. If a woman has many male friends, then she will have back up plans for emotional revenge in fights. If a woman has gay male friends, then she will be encouraged to be open about her sexuality and will pursue a more playful view of sexual fun on her nights out.

What does a woman do in her free time? If she is always going out to bars and clubs is a woman who is full of sexual chaos. She is addicted to sexual attention and that will come back to haunt a man later.

Is she politically radical? There are radical feminists who will be more challenging to frame than less radicalized women. A radical feminist will get off on argument/confrontation and will make a point to test a man beyond what a normal woman would. Her ideology is less based on female empowerment and more based on male hatred. Why would a man want to be associated with a woman who mocks male leadership? These women are best avoided as their political ideology has become a religion to them. Is a woman on a lot of anti-psychotic medications and how many cats does she have? These are all warning to a woman's mental stability. What is the initial attraction with a woman? Many women will go on dates with men whom they know they will friendzone. These women will use these men for free dinners and dates when they are bored. They will string these men along as playthings while seeking stronger men on the side. Progress physical interactions to test whether a woman is friend zoning. Do not associate with women unless it is romantic leading. Anything else is exploitation and damaging to masculine pride.

  The key to vetting a woman for quality is to pay attention to a woman's history and speech. Women reveal themselves easily but will hide if they feel judgment. When dating a woman, a man should encourage a woman to be completely honest with him in a "Judgement free zone" – Judge her hidden and this will encourage her to open up. A woman hates holding secrets and wants to share herself to a man. Women will tell a man the most vulgar aspects of their being if a man is showing that he is non-judgmental in asking. Ask about her history and then do not show judgment on the face. A woman will reveal her past and her viewpoints on sexual matters easily because women hate holding back expression. Remember, women encourage expression and open communication because it eases their own anxiety since they rely on others for emotional regulation. This is why asking key questions to see if a woman will open up about her sexual past while showing a spirit of NONJUDGMENT will encourage the woman to show her hand. Once her hand is shown the man can place his bets on whether or not he wants to invest in a woman if her loyalty will be in doubt.

Where can a man find a quality woman? Everywhere. Sometimes socially shy women will be online. Women are shopping for groceries. Women are browsing at bookstores. Women are in churches. Go to a greenery and buy a plant for your home. Look around, there will be women there. If there is not a ring on a woman's wedding finger then approach her. Ask her for her opinion on a matter related to the environment and be playful with her answer. The most overthought aspect of game/dating with men is finding women. The world is full of women and women love shopping. Go to places where they either shop or pray. Women love going out and being seen. And women like to be approached romantically because women like having their egos raised.

Negotiations

win

the

game

Women are innately aware of the power of negotiation. They have to be as the weaker physical gender. This causes them to rely on speech as the mechanism for control and negotiation through speech as means to power. While women are innately aware of this from a young age, young boys are sold false enlightenment through chivalry. Young boys are told they already hold the power so that relinquishing it will be seen as a further display of strength. And this was how I too felt as an unframed young man growing up. I was told in one ear that men were vulgar brutes and that being obsessed with power was weak in the other ear. This was mind control by the weaker sex. But while they may be physically weaker, they are more cunning and manipulative. What greater way to win a battle than to convince the other side to set down their weapons for a "Fair fight" – See? Women will psychologically disempower men by having them moralize "Being above power dynamics" But what a man must realize is that a woman never surrenders her own obsession with power dynamics. She moralizes her own manipulative powers while telling men to demonize their own. This gaslighting approach is highly effective because men are idealistic and easily controlled by shame tactics. They have been groomed in emotionalism which allows women to control them with guilt strategy. Emotion is a spell cast that ensnares for control. And pay very closely to the following words. Everything is about power and control. Everything is a game and everything is a negotiation within the games. When a man is sex starved in a relationship or is not getting his sexual desires met; what is the first think I think about him? He is a bad negotiator. Whether a man works in a corporation, making deals for his own business or in a relationship with a woman; it is all power plays. I can hear the critics already and what do they say? "But Jerr, that is not romance" Wrong. Making a woman horny is romance. Building arousal is romance. Being a proud masculine leader over a woman is romance. Being sexually fulfilled is romance. *The false propaganda nowadays is that a man's surrender is romance.* That to give a woman everything she desires and to forsake our desires is romance. Do you see? We are told that men transferring their power to women is romance. And this is why feminism grows while my forgotten generation of fatherless men are further disempowered. We are exploited for our ignorance by a world that feeds on our desperate state. We have too many struggling orphaned men in the world. The pain is too much. We must start teaching men to negotiate for power with women. We must empower men before they further sink into despair. This is why I write.

What negotiations will a man see in the early stages of sexual selection? If a man sets up a date at a location that is near him maybe the woman will respond that the location is too far for her. What can a man do in this scenario? He can alter the location a little closer to the woman.

The initial ask is greed and then inch a step away from the initial greed. This allows what we call a false choice and shows compromise which smooths negotiations. The ask must be greedy and then we step back from the greed. Most guys are too timid to ask for their true desires and so they easily give away their power to women When a man is asking for a raise, he may ask for more than he truly desires because it allows his employer to compromise to his initial wants. See? That is negotiation basics. It applies to business, war and sex. All things are in constant conflict and battle. Birth and death. Growth and decay. Eating and digestion. The reality of all things. And we must accept reality to manipulate reality. What men need to realize is that women love men who are good at negotiations because they are seeking a masculine leader who is a master of reality. Women love being manipulated because they seek a strong manipulator to pair with.

A man should be gaining ground in domination over a woman the more he is associating with her. In the early stages of sexual selection women have more power. This is why a man should be careful about being overly dominant in the early stages and learn "Smooth compromises" as described previously. The heart of desire within a man must expand daily/weekly/monthly/yearly in a relationship with a woman. His dominance should be growing and her submission should be growing. A man should learn the basics of masculine frame which I wrote about in The Wall Speaks. Frame is a negotiation tool that projects power. But what a man needs to understand that this is the truth of romance. Think. What do women want above all else? Fun. And what do women hate above all else? Boredom. Women get off on conflict and struggle. This struggle for power is a game that makes relationships stimulating for them. When a man is "content" with his current power position and does not have anything further to fight for is stagnation and dull. And it shows not just dullness but weakness in seeking desire. It is like the man who preaches simplicity only because he fears complexity. A slave who worships the bars of his prison cell only because he fears liberation. Women know that a man has desire that he is either too afraid to seek or too weak to fight for. That is why thinking about constant negotiations in the early stages of sexual selection is healthy for romance and strengthens relationships once they form.

A leader is not leading unless he is directing. And which direction should he be leading a woman to? His desires and passions. What most unframed men do not realize is that women get sexually aroused by losing negotiations. As long as the loss of negotiation is "Smooth" and not clunky. For example, if a man asks a woman to send him a sexy picture as a way to flirt and she asks him to send her a sexy pic is a shit test for negotiation. "Send me one first and I'll send you one" would be one way to smooth way to negotiate. Or if the woman already sent a sexy pic and she says "Now your turn" The man can say "Send me another one and I'll send you something special" See? It is about always being the winner of a negotiation even in compromise. This is charisma and the art of negotiation. Men who do not compromise at all will come off as awkward which will kill chemistry with most women. Women want to lose negotiations but they want to lose while keeping some dignity. And a man who smoothly wins negotiations is allowing the woman a false victory.

This is key for understanding how a relationship forms and how it unfolds through time. A man who wants everything up front will most times blow up sexual selection opportunities. Men must slowly make power gains over a woman through time like an anaconda wrapping around its prey. Slow game. The game is revealed if greed is overbearing. That is why a man must hide his greed while expanding it through the relationship. Take five steps forward and two steps back. Take five steps forward and two steps back. Take five steps forward and one step back. Take five steps forward. And before a woman realizes it, she will be far from her original position.

Women will get with men that they think they can change because they believe in everything that I have written. They already believe in the power of negotiation and they believe in power dynamics. It is men who are fooled into giving up power in order for women to win negotiations. And there can be many reasons why this is encouraged in our society. Women of course want power but why would men also encourage male disempowerment? Maybe a man was abused by other men. Maybe a man has daughters that he wants to win negotiations. There are many reasons why fellow men would disempower other men through false advice and media propaganda.

When a man is in the early stages of a sexual selection, a woman will be far from his fundamental beliefs and desires. But remember that a woman will form herself around a man the more she is emotionally attached to him and the stronger his frame is around her. A woman is an empty vessel that seeks being filled by a man's authority. This is why a man should not be overly provocative or truthful of his views of reality in the early stages of sexual selection. A radical feminist could slowly form herself around a proud man given enough frame control and time. *Five steps forward, two steps back.* All women can be framed but some women require more frame. For example, one woman can be five steps forward one step back while a radical feminist may be five steps forward and four steps back. Both are power gains but one may be easier than the other. It just means whether or not the man wants to pursue a more challenging woman who requires more effort to frame. The key thing is to establish dominance and to influence the woman with your will.

Cooking

the

frog

slow

The more a man takes his time with a woman in the beginning stages of attraction the more her arousal will build. Inexperienced men will show their full hand of desire which will ruin attraction. They will move too quick too soon and scare women away. A woman knows a man wants to fuck. And when a man hides that desire only fuels arousal more so. That is why slow game works. Hiding sexual intent in the beginning enhances attraction will causes woman to invest herself with the man for the eventual sexual intent. A lot of men are so sexually desperate and think female arousal works the same as their own which compels them to show their sexual intent early which makes the frog jump out of the cooking pot of desire. What does it mean to walk around a park holding hands and kissing a woman goodbye? Sugar makes the medicine go down. And this sweet approach increases physical arousal in women. It comes from a basic understanding of female nature. First that women are surrounded by sexually thirsty men and are overwhelmed by this mundane reality. When a man hides his sexual intent sets him apart from the average man while fueling mystery about his intent. The key is to keep things short and sweet. A thirty-minute walk around the park and a kiss goodbye. Short and sweet. Also, this costs very little money which helps many men since dating can get costly. Women just want to be led around by the hand and kissed. That does not require a fancy dinner date. Take her by the hand, lead her by the hand, lead the conversation and then cut the date short because you are projecting your busyness. Leave her wanting. This just turned up the heat under her. She will be thinking about the mystery behind the man. What is he hiding and what is his intent? To hide intent is to spark fantasy. A few short and sweet dates will prime a woman for wanting more. Or it could be going to a bar in a walkable district. Get a drink, go on a brief walk afterwards and kiss her goodnight. A man should touch a woman's dreams before he touches her body. This will wrap her around his finger. Women fall in love not through reality but through fantasy. A woman craves mystery because a woman craves to use her feminine intuition to unpack a mystery. This is one reason why women love murder mysteries and true crime. It allows them to put on a detective hat to solve a mystery. (This is one reason of many why women love true crime shows and something I will write more in depth in future)

But while a man is hiding his sexual intent, he should be conditioning a woman to his physical touch. This will make her think about sex without talking about it. It is holding hands, hugging and a kiss. All these things fuel romantic passions inside a woman's mind when she is separated from the man. And this conditioning should start on the first date otherwise the woman will think the man awkward and not mysterious. Hug the woman upon meeting up and direct her to the seat. Find ways to touch her arm and hands during conversation. Take her by the hand when walking to her car after date. Kiss her good night and place hands on her hips. See? This is low sexual display but enough to fuel sexual arousal in a woman. A man should not talk sex in the early dates with a woman. His subtle touches will be enough to make a woman think about sex. It gets the point across in a smooth way and not like an inexperienced boy.

Take the big things slow and sprinkle small escalations over the experience. A woman is protective by nature and that is why a man must get past layer upon layer of defenses through smooth manipulations. And these "Smooth manipulations" are exactly what women do to men but in different ways. That is why a man should feel zero guilt in in his method of manipulation. There are only two modes of being in existence. We either manipulate or are being manipulated. Women gaslight men into believing in a utopian vision where everybody is in equal control and nobody manipulates. That is a supreme lie for power. But women do not feel bad lying because they first lie to themselves and then sell "Their truth" – They want to believe in a world where nobody is fighting for power and so they gaslight men this thought while gaining power over them.

After a sugar sweet date, a man should drag a woman for a period to make her think about whether or not he genuinely likes her. Nobody is the biggest killer of romance than men who cannot handle distance after dates. These men will message a woman right after saying "Had a good time" or will message a woman the next day "Good morning beautiful" – What they are doing is ruining the arousal they built up on the preceding experience. Letting a woman have alone time with the experience is where her fantasy builds. She herself will turn up the heat that will eventually "Cook the frog" –

A

woman

wants

what

she

must

not

have

The vast amount of power being held in human reality is based not on overwhelming truth but on overwhelming belief which is vastly different. Assumption of power proceeds power. People will be ready to bend the knee to the one who walks like a king. It is human nature. We know that those above us act with measurement/discipline while those below us act in chaos/undiscipline. Is this truth? Those above us are just like us but there we given the gift of self-belief along with wealth. A king's son will act different than a pauper's son. The gift is not just the throne of power itself but the presentation of self.

Framed confidence is power wrapped in mystery. The more a man projects power with masculine frame, the more a woman will invest herself in interest to him. Why? Because she wants to know why the man seems as confident in his power as he does. She wants to see the power source. She wants to look behind the curtain to The Wizard of Oz. She wants to eat the forbidden fruit in the garden. The fruit of the knowledge of good and bad. The eternal mystery of all things. A woman is innately attracted to mystery/power which is how men have gamed women since the beginning. Want to attract a woman? Become the forbidden fruit in the garden of her imagination. Become the fruit that she must not touch. Become the mystery in the center of the garden. A woman seeks what she must not seek. She seeks to be dispelled. She seeks the cure to her fascination which is ultimate knowing. That is why women condition men to open up and express themselves. Women want men to demystify themselves which transfers the power. A bitten forbidden fruit that loses taste as soon as it is eaten. It falls to the ground after consumed and left abandoned to rot. It was the same in the Garden of Eden and it is the same in romance. A woman is tempted by the darkness that is held out of her sight and not the spotlight of what is already known.

This is the fundamental concepts of frame and game. And both involve getting a woman to chase her own fantasy. Game shifts to frame. Game involves a presentation of a man's energy/world and removal of them. This presentation and removal are like dancing forward and dancing back. Pursuit and chase. In the beginning of sexual selection, women hold more power because they are the choosers of sexual selection. But this power gradually shifts to the man after he displays the fun/power/mystery. Once a woman is possessed by the desire in her heart, she will forsake everything just like Eve. The object of her desire will become the sole concern in her mind. That is why a confident presentation of power and dragging a woman after she is introduced gets her chasing.

This is why once a man traps a woman in her own desire, he can start pulling away his attention and affection. This usually comes after the "Flake period" early in romance and after a physical investment has been made or established psychological investment. Give a woman what she desires. Give her fun, attention and affection. Then pull it away. Become distant. While frame is essential always, there is marked transition from game to frame alone in the relationship process with a woman. Game is fun while frame is doubt. Doubt is the glue that keeps a woman attached to a man. And a man who knows how to manipulate a woman's innate doubt will build deep attachment.

In the beginning when establishing a connection with a woman should be more communicative than later stages. For example, if a man is using 2/3 words or messages or less than a woman in the beginning; he will shift it to 2/5 once emotional attachment/investment is established. This is creating more distance for arousal to build which is like blowing on the embers of a small fire. Creating distance is like pulling the tree of knowledge of good and bad from Eve's hands and leading her where you want. The object of desire must be removed and distanced from the seeker to increase investment. How? Why would a woman be trying so hard unless she believed the man to be a prize? See? Doubt works on a woman because a woman is controlled by ego. The same ego that led Eve astray to desire to be like God by knowing the mystery. How does a woman's mind work? I'll recreate inner dialogue "This man is framed. I wonder what he is thinking. He sure seems confident in himself. Ill test him a few times... He passed the tests with calm charisma. His power is real. I'm curious about him. He kissed me. Good kiss. I would not kiss a loser, so he is special. He is more dominant than other guys, normally I would not be this submissive but he makes it easy and it is fun. I'm getting excited"

To understand a woman, think in reverse. A woman protects her ego after the fact. This is where a man's boldness in seeking physical engagement will increase his favor because a woman must defend herself from shame. In a way, a woman will sleep with a loser but will deem him a winner afterwards. See? It is ego protection. And then she will deem him a loser if the connection falls apart. Again, ego protection. We protect our ego investments because we must make sense of our choices and we must defend the choices we make. And no one does this more than a woman since she is ruled by ego. The more a woman associates her ego with a man the greater his image will become. She will paint his image with the grandest and broadest brush strokes of fantasy because he is her choice. Women chase men who are not interested in them because women are curious about men who believe themselves better. Distance and disinterest are the tools of romance. And these tools can be used as soon as a woman is initially ensnared by her heart. Then she can be led to wherever the man wants to lead her to. This is the rules of love. It is up to each individual man to realize when to start applying more distance to increase arousal. Each situation is different and each woman's ego is different. But they all share the same commonalties of the rules of attraction.

Performance

anxiety

A man sinks when he forgets to swim. When a man becomes hyper aware of self when publicly speaking, he will freeze and stutter. Performance anxiety comes in all flavors and they are a restriction on the spirit. What good is a man's arms and legs; if he forgets to use them to save himself in water? What good is the greatest speech ever written if a man nervously reads it in a stutter before others? See? It is the performance itself which transfers the truth of our being. We must carry ourself with confidence to inspire confidence. And it is the confident projection that fuels our own confidence. One foot over the other and we are running. Act confident, see the trust on others faces and become emboldened in confidence. The act fuels the act. Confidence breeds confidence.

This is the same in romance and sex. A man must be confident in his desires otherwise he will be controlled by the desires of others. To be a leader is to lead in self-belief. Nothing kills sexual chemistry more than a man showing his nerves. This applies to being on a date and being in the bedroom. Nervous energy breeds nervous energy. Remember, a woman is a mojo leach and psychic vampire. She surfs on whatever energy the man creates. And how a man handles himself will be how a woman handles him. How does a man handle himself in failure? Does he spotlight it with attention and shame? Or does he ignore the failure altogether. For example, if a man is fucking and finishes sooner than he wanted, what does he do? Does he say to the woman "Sorry, this rarely happens to me...", or does he say nothing, roll off the bed and leave the woman thinking in doubt?

In sex and romance it is best to leave the woman in doubt about herself than to bring attention to our own failures. For example, if the man finishes sex before he wants to, is it because he is a premature ejaculator or is it because he just wanted to finish early? If the man is struggling for a hard erection, is it because he lacks confidence or is it because he lacks arousal over the woman? See? Cast the light of doubt to the woman not with words but with the absence of explanation. When nothing is said, a woman will stand in doubt of herself which will free the man of his own failures.

Should a man with ED date? Of course, he should. He should be emotionally detached from the experience and see what happens. In failure, leave the woman in doubt and move on. What could be causing ED in a man? Porn strips a man of erotic imagination which fuels his erection. Think about how the cock works. It works based on imaginative will and bodily health. When a man cannot be aroused by subtle signs then he will be reliant on hardcore manifestations. His arousal gets softer and softer the more he requires to stimulate himself. Porn ultimately castrates a man and makes his dick rot. Push away porn and go say "Hi" to a woman. Do not soften the cock through vulgar viewing of other men fucking. It is bad for cock and bad for masculine pride. But a cock can be rebuilt. Protect the eye from all erotic stimulation and summon the power of erotic imagination. Only imagination and touch. Soon the cock will regain power when the erotic imagination is strengthened. Then a man will realize how important imaginative will is to his own arousal. And will be more protective of stripping himself of that imaginative willpower in the future.

Free the self of performance anxiety. Do not fear failure. Fear inaction. There is a great quote by FDR "The only thing we have to fear is fear itself" It is fear that freezes our steps and it is fear that makes us stumble in action. Fear breeds fear. The fear on our face will embolden those around us into authority. A nervous man on a date with a woman creates a brave woman. Whomever is showing fear emboldens the others. And vice versa.

That is why confidence should lead the way for a man. When he stumbles, he should correct himself with grace and move on. It is not the failure that ruins a man, it is how he handles himself in failure. A woman understands that life and leadership are imperfect. It is the charisma of transcending failure that calms a woman into submission. She does not expect perfect, she expects a man who makes others forget his imperfections. Do not worry about failing. Just put a brave face on and give it a valiant effort.

The

anxiety

in

a

man's

heart

     We will continue to discuss performance anxiety because nothing else plagues a man's success in life and romance more than performance anxiety. It is a man's nerves that get the best of him in approach/dating which spills the drink of desire in his own hands. Many men let their anxiety overwhelm them into impotence. For example, if a man gets morning erections, then he has a healthy cock. But this same man can have difficulty in performing sex because he has performance anxiety. In The Wall Speaks, I wrote about three archetypes of unframed individuals. A raging bull, flighty bird and my own archetype of a paralyzed deer. My archetype is like a deer frozen before headlights. It is paralysis of spirit. What does it mean when a man cannot urinate before others in a restroom? What does it mean when a man can urinate in a restroom alone but cannot when his boss enters the restroom? This is a perceptional prison of the man's own making. He builds the walls of his own prison that prevents him from relaxing enough for movement. This freezes him into himself. This can be the same for a man who has more confidence over unattractive women than attractive women. Why would a man become nervous over one but not the other? This perceptional shift creates doubt in self. It is the doubt in self that creates performance anxiety. What happens when a man surrenders to doubt in self? Those that surround him will be emboldened against him. This is the same for a man in business, war and romance. *When man gets performance anxiety with a woman, she then gets performance enhancement.* One fuels the other and it either spirals a man into failure or rockets him to success depending on which side he is on.

Since performance anxiety is based on lacking belief in self, how can a man strengthen his sense of self? He should practice masculine frame which increases certainty of self (My book The Wall Speaks explains in depth)

There is a trick to public speaking that makes more sense when a man understands the framework for performance anxiety. It is based on the common nightmare of being naked before others. Why would being naked before others cause fear? It is singular exposure of shame for others judgment. See? We fear that others know our fears. And the trick to public speaking? To picture the entire audience as naked. It is reverse of the judgment position. Who sits on the throne, them or you? This is what it means to have a perceptional shift. Who is nervous a man on a date or the woman? When a man is driving to a date, he must tell himself "She will be more nervous than me" – This will prime his perception for that fact. The longer he holds frame in the first five minutes of date the more that fact will reveal itself as truth. We set the frame for others to think from otherwise we think from the frame they set. Who is the judge over whom?

A woman is a compliment to a man and she knows which role to fulfil in the first interactions with the man. And whatever the frame he sets up in the first engagements will either make his desires easier to fulfil or more challenging to attain. Women will say to themselves "This guy is more dominant... being submissive with him could be fun" Or women will think "This guy is weak. I'll have to be more dominant. But I could use the guy for my needs" – Now if a guy is unframed and weak in the early stages of sexual selection then he will encounter more push back when he attempts domination. The woman became emboldened in her authority over the man and any attempt at him establishing authority will encounter more doubt. Not only do first appearances set a frame inside a person's mind but first interactions set the frame of authority. This is why it is crucial for a man set the frame for his own masculine leadership from approach to first date. It will make any relationship that builds from that point on much easier for him.

How can a man overcome his own performance anxiety? He must BECOME CERTAIN IN THE ROLE HE IS FULFILING. For example, a father will summon bravery because he does not want to frighten his children. Would he show fear without children? Maybe. But he does not allow the fear to overtake him because he does not want to spread fear. When we view reality split between leader and follower is a boost to our own confidence. And that confidence boost dispels the mental roadblocks that freeze us within ourselves. Let us go back to the man who cannot urinate because his boss walked in the restroom. If the man is quitting his job, would he still feel this way? No. He would relax into the authority of himself and not fear the authority of the other. See? It is best to have a relaxed mind to relax the body. And the way to do this is by flipping authority in the mind. Also, when we "Play loose" we do not become restricted by fear. What does "Play loose" mean? It means that we do not overly fear failure When a man over concerns himself with failure is what creates the failure before it can be realized. It is like missing a shot at an oncoming bear because we fear to miss it. What sense would that make? We shoot our shot because we only get one life. This is why a man should not overly concern himself with failure. Make mistakes. Make lots of mistakes. Let the mistakes desensitize the spirit until it is calloused. Desensitization therapy is key for men who wind themselves up in their minds. Afraid of talking to women? Talk to more women. Afraid of being nervous on a date? Go on many dates. The more a man detaches from failure the more he will find success. Our mind is the greatest prison on earth. *But our mind also is the greatest liberator on earth.* Flip the mind in your favor before you are dead.

A

woman

wants

a

feeling

Women are ruled by emotion which allows them to pair bond. Emotionalism increases the more someone uses others as external validators of their inner realities. A woman is inherently reliant on others because her hormone flux creates a spiraling uncertainty of self within that causes her to seek out others to reaffirm her sense of self. This high emotionalism that exists in women allows them to emotionally attach themselves to men. And how does a man get a woman to emotionally attach herself to him? He must incite emotion wrapped in mystery before dragging it away from the woman. This will get the woman spinning the wheels of her imagination about the man which invests her time into him. The more a man incites and withdraws; the more the woman will begin chasing his affection. The key is to leave a woman wanting more. This requires a man to know when to cut things short. To cut short means to leave wanting. That is why brief encounters increase the more fantasy. Fill in the blank. Mystery is based on partial knowledge. A man who leaves a woman wrapped in a warm feeling after a fun time will get her wanting to reexperience that moment again. The flames of passion are based on allowing a woman to build her own narrative about her romance. And the less a man reveals about himself the more woman will be interested in him. But remember, the core aspect of romance between men/women is based on a woman seeking a masculine leader. Who is busy? Leaders. This is why cutting encounters short will spike interest. A man and woman can have good chemistry but the more they spend time together on the initial dates will dispel the fantasy of arousal. How long should a date be? It could be thirty minutes; it could be an hour or two. But the key is to cut it short at the point where the woman is having the most fun. That is the time to say "Okay. I'll walk you to your car" Or "Lets plan date two" --- The woman will be riding high on fun and will want to experience again.

Women prize fun above all else. And what is fun to a woman? Being led around by a framed man she is getting attention from. The key to a woman's heart is to release butterflies in her stomach. A small nervous anxiety like a person about to ride a rollercoaster. Women love not just positive emotion but negative emotion. *It is the movement of emotion that is prized in a woman's heart.* This is what feminized men do not realize. They try to just give a woman positive reassurance which smothers sexual arousal. Spike a woman's interest and then leave her in doubt. Have a fun time with a woman and then drag her in mystery. Drop into a woman's life, make her feel alive and then exit. See? It is the dance of love. Manipulative? Just as manipulative as nice guys giving flowers, compliments and gifts to woman. But this is actually effective because it showcases power of authority. The supreme authority of not needing a woman. Nice guys reek in desperation which smothers the distance required to flame the passions of love. Life is rhythm. And exiting on a good note leaves a woman entranced in a feeling she'll want to experience again. For example, right after a conversation high note/laugh/chemistry is the time to leave her wanting. This requires a man to pay attention to higher notes of excitement compared to the average moments within a date/experience. When a man leaves a woman high, she will carry that feeling for the rest of the day and into the next. It will follow her for days and weeks. Then a man returns to give the woman the same feeling like a drug dealer of emotion. This framework goes back to our ancestral memory when men used to leave women for long periods of time for hunt/war. A woman expects a man to drop in and drop out. That is the rhythm of romance. If a woman is hanging around a group of men and they are all chatting together; it will be the man who makes a special appearance, spikes the excitement and then leaves because he must that will leave the woman enchanted. Spike of interest and withdrawal of interest. This is sexual chemistry basics. This is why when a man has a good date with a man, he should not destroy the moment by narrating the experience or revealing his feelings about the experience too soon. For example, after a date, a man should just smile and say goodbye to a woman. Many awkward guys will say "Had a good time" "Did you enjoy yourself?" or pepper the ending with awful spice of revelation of intent. What does it mean when a woman has a good time with a man and he says "Okay" before standing up with a "I'll walk you to the car" – Before kissing her and then saying a simple "Bye" – See? *What could this mean?* What is the man thinking? – Let these questions exist in the woman's mind and let her ponder on the mystery within. Then she will be chasing the man in her dreams. And it is through dream that romance becomes red hot in flames. It is through mystery where a man gains power. It is through distance that a man gets the reins of power. Get close and then pull back. Let her ache and pine for you. Let her fill her mind with your image. Let her paint her fantasy and seek recapturing that feeling once again.

Getting

past

a

woman's

armor

Women emotionally protect themselves because emotional loss is painful to them. They do not want to pair bond and then be abandoned. This is why the more a woman has experience with men the higher her guard against attachment will be. But is through emotional attachment where a man attains power over the woman in the relationship. Why? Because she does not want to lose her attachment. This is the key to a healthy relationship dynamic. Anybody who doubts this is fooling himself. We have lived in a time where women get more and more power over men while initiating 3/4ths of all divorces in my nation. The "Give a woman everything she says she desires" is supreme falsehood that is creating chaos in our nations. Weak men who attempt a Hollywood version of romance will be cucked. And men who think that the best way to control women is through violence are tyrants who deserve to fall. The middle way is best. We do not simp for women and we do not physically force women. See? The middle way is to get a woman emotionally attached and then frame her. The power must shift further to the man's side the further the couple are in a relationship together. This will decrease chaos and increase stability in romance. When a woman slowly invests herself in her man, she will be more willing to sacrifice her previous self to better compliment her leader's self. *Love is loss of self.* A woman who falls in love is a woman who loses sense of her own self because she wants the vessel of herself to be filled by the object of her desire. This is how our species is able to pair bond for mating ever since the beginning. It is emotional attachment that allows feminize submission and that submission allows a woman to compliment herself to her man's will. Many men do not know how to get women to emotionally invest in them and therefore have no true power in their relationships. What do you want in romance? What is the desire that is not being fulfilled that you want fulfilled? A woman will be more apt to give a man what he desires when she fears losing what fills her vessel. Women IN love are IN possession of their men. They are entranced by a spell of their own making. They crave their men like drugs and they fear losing that feeling. It is this fear of loss that allows a woman to submit herself to her man. And it is emotional attachment that is the chains of desire that keeps her bonded under his frame. When a man who knows how to get a woman to think about him is a man who knows how to build attachment. We take up residence in the minds of women to grow in power. Then once there is emotional attachment, we can lead our women like slaves of desire to the direction of our passion. And a woman who is heavily guarded emotionally is a woman who requires slower romance. She requires a man to hide his intent even more with her. She requires more spiking of interest and more dragging in mystery. The methods stay the same but must be inflated for greater effect because the woman herself has become desensitized by over experience. These "battle hardened" women require more game to get underneath their armor. But once a man has them in the palm of his hand then he can manipulate just like the rest. Remember, excite in person before cutting it short followed by occasional correspondence to set up the next encounter. This peppering effect will keep a woman dreaming about the man who makes her feel something. And a woman who does not feel is not alive.

Slow

inflates

imagination

A common issue with men with women is that they become overly excited which dispels attraction. These men are like hummingbirds of awkwardness that ruin the sweet chemistry before them. What does it mean to be overly excited? It means to project fear. It means to dispel imagination with overwhelming truth. The truth of nerves and this nervous energy makes a woman more nervous. Women feed on energy. And a man who can calm his nerves is a man who can calm a woman's nerves. What does a woman do with a nervous man? She becomes anxious and this anxiety it the motivation that causes her to overcome that anxiety by carrying the frame the man abandons. This is why nervous men create careful women. The shared negative emotion creates a lost feeling that is resolved by overcoming the man's nerves. Women become emboldened by weak men. It is the projection of weakness that creates the strength.

What a man must realize is how much power and control he has over every aspect of his being. A man can control how wide his eye lids open. Think about that. Look in the mirror and notice how wide the eyes look when speaking. The wider the eye the more excited in anxiety a man will look. To close the eyelid slightly is to show mastery of control and power of self. The same for speech. How fast does a man speak? Is he like a dog eating his food quickly because he is afraid that it will be taken from him? This flight response will quicken speech and actions. And women are repelled by men who are stuck in flight mode because the mode itself is based on fear. That is why fast talker guys create bad chemistry. But besides quickness in expression which projects anxiety of self; it also robs a woman of her imagination. *Slowing down expression, speeds up fantasy.* Think about it like this. Women love using their feminine intuition. And this means that women presume to know not only what a man is thinking but how to finish his thoughts. The faster we go in behavior the more we rob someone of the capacity to complete the meaning of our expressions. We live in a world of ego and nobody holds the jewel of ego like a woman. An unframed man speaks fast, walks fast and eats fast. He is like an anxious dog and he shows his fear to all. When a man slows his speech and movements is power projection; power over his self that showcases his measured control. This power over self is the opposite of fear. We move slow because we are in confidence of self and environment. This calm reassurance eases a woman into our frames. But it also allows a woman to "Fill in the gaps" with her imagination. Why does dancing slow project more charisma than dancing fast? Because we do not overextend our hand beyond our current competence and we allow others to speed us up in their minds with their imaginations. The same for speech. A man who speaks slow pulls the listeners ears closer to him. They await in anticipation for him to finish his thought. And what are they doing while they are listening to him? They are finishing his thought in their mind. It is an expansion of fantasy based on the slowness of receiving information. This is one aspect of what is means to be "Smooth" – Our image is smooth in others projection because our behaviors are slowed down. And a man may think they he is being boring by going slow and that speeding up behavior would make him somehow more interesting. This is not true. The average man is talking/moving much faster than he thinks. And a man who slows himself down most times is not going "Slow" but rather slowing himself into a normalize state. How many men are affected by the flight/fight response that speeds up their behaviors? More than we think. Many guys have anxiety issues from early chronic childhood stress or from an acute event that destabilized their sense of self. They have been conditioned into a state of fear that shakes their cage of self. These men do not realize that their behaviors reflect their subconscious fears. Maybe they romanticize this fear state as their "True identity" and think that people who go slow are "Boring" – These men are ignorant of the women's perception. Slowness is power projection and power is the greatest aphrodisiac to women. A man who hurries himself is either anxious from an internal reason to himself or he is overly affected by the pressures that surround him. Maybe a young boy was told to quicken his step from an overbearing father. "Pick it up boy" See? A man may be conditioned into pauper's behavior because he was never taught the behavior of a king. Who needs to hurry himself, the servant or the master? This is why a man should practice slowing his behavior to not only project power but to project mystery around that power source. And women are attracted to not just power itself but the hidden reason for the power like Eve to the forbidden fruit. It is the mystery behinds a man's confidence that pulls a woman into his frame. The power is the clue and she will follow it because she too wants the power. And what is the power of expression? It is our imaginative will. We think and therefore become. What does it mean to lower the eye lid by a few centimeters because this is a power projection? It is mastery of self and awareness of how we are perceived. Not just awareness of how we are perceived but how our own projection influences the thinking in others. We set the frame of thought for others to think inside. If a man carries himself like a king, then others will be more apt to kneel at the throne when he sits. He first must play the part for the others to join the reality. And the more a man slows his behaviors the more conscious a woman will become over her anxious behaviors. A slow masculine energy creates a buzzing high feminine energy in women. This polarity creates romantic energy as the woman's self-consciousness feeling makes her primed to be in qualification mode to the one who projects power.

A

man

hides

his

intent

What most men need to realize is how overwhelmed by sexual thirst women are by surrounding men. Sex is the obvious intent of men in sexual selection. And to hide that sexual intent is to fuel mystery. This is why slow romance spikes intrigue and arousal. What does slow romance mean? It means that a man must not rush the woman into his obvious sexual hunger. He must lead her in a connection while hiding that intent. The more he sidelines the sexual intent the more the woman will think about him. And getting a woman to think about a man is the greatest challenge in the beginning stages of sexual selection. For a man to expand himself within the mind of a woman requires him to showcase his difference from the rest of competing men. A woman wants a man who stands apart from the group because a woman wants a leader who is not controlled by groupthink. This is one reason that women judge men based on how similar they are in approach/dating to the next man. And to stand apart from the rest of men is to secure a seat in the fantasy of a woman's mind. How can a man set himself apart from the mediocre masses? He must showcase that he has not only power of presentation through frame but power of control over his sexual urges. But while he is hiding his sexual thirst, he should be fueling the woman's sexual thirst. To do this, a man must be making a woman think about sex subconsciously and not consciously. A man who takes a woman on sweet dates will increase her sexual thirst. Instead of revealing the vulgar intent on the first date, it can be dragged out in a tease over a few dates. The physical escalation increases in slow arousal. This allows the woman to leave the date in her own sexual want and fantasize about the man in dream. And it is through dream that romance shines the brightest. Getting a woman to dream about us is the key to their hearts. And a woman only thinks about mystery. "Does this man think I am attractive?" The woman will think when a man delays his sex impulse which increase her doubt enough to condition her for qualification mode. "Why is this guy not drooling his sexual thirst over me?" The woman will think when the man is the one pushing off sex. Whomever holds the power in sex, holds the power in the relationship. And a man who makes a woman wait for sex is a man who assumes authority over her.

But "Slow romance" does something highly sexual with women, it teases them. And women loved to be teased. What does it mean to tease? It means to dangle the delight of passion before someone who thirsts for it. What does it mean to kiss a woman soft? What does it mean to pull away slightly when a woman pushes her lips forward? What does it mean to brush the lips softly against a woman's lips and gently against her neck? What does it mean to touch the small of a woman's back and to glide the hand around everywhere but the most obvious? See? This is sexual teasing without sex. It is circling the banquet of fatty dishes without taking a seat. To understand sexual teasing is to understand a woman's sexual biology. A woman's genitalia is out of her sight which fuels her imagination and spreads out her sexual arousal over her entire body. The basics of psychology are built atop biology. Women crave mystery because their own sexuality is a mystery to them. And a woman must be prepared for penetration by arousing herself enough for lubrication. To arouse a woman is to understand that sexuality is everywhere and not just the most obvious. A kiss. A soft breath on the back of the neck. A gentle caress around a woman's body without touching the obvious erogenous zones. This circling and teasing around the obvious is what spikes a woman's erotic imagination. It is taking the road less traveled that ultimately brings the greater adventure. And this is the truth with a woman's body. It is also true in a man's approach and dates with a woman. *To circle the desire is to frame the desire in mind.* A man who wants to touch a woman's breast but instead circles his fingers around without getting to the core of his desire is flaming arousal. Men who want to understand how women become aroused need to understand that mystery with teasing of that mystery is what make the waters of passion pour forth. This subverting of expectation increases anticipation and anticipation is what releases dopamine in our brains. A woman knows what to expect with men and a man who alters his strategy will shine the brightest among them. But this teasing is only appreciated when the opportunity can be seized. For example, an unframed man who is nervous with a woman will be expected to be cowardly in his desires. His boldness would be more helpful than teasing.

But the man who has the bird in his hand and allows it to fly away free will be the one who incites the most interest. It is a spirit of abundance in not capitalizing on a moment. When a man tries to get everything, he can on a date with a woman will blend himself into the mediocre masses while showing the desperation of his sexual thirst. A man who hides his sexual thirst will drink in abundance when he leads the woman to the oasis beyond the moment. Remember that all women like Eve want to know the mystery behind the power source. And a display of power over the self intrigues them into following us to where we want to lead them. They must know the mystery of the power and it exists behind a man's closed lips. Do not let a woman know the plan. Let her think about her own reasons for the slow romance. Just as a frog in cold water will surrender to the heat, a woman will surrender when the sexual heat is finally raised after acclimation from the hidden intent.

The key thing for a man to remember is that a woman is a walking erogenous zone. Her clit out of sight spreads pleasure beyond her sight. Do not be obvious in touch. A woman already knows whether or not she will surrender sexually to a man within the first five minutes of meeting. Then after that, everything is foreplay to the eventual culmination of flesh. A man who could ravish a woman but instead softly moves his fingers over the soft line of her jaw before kissing her goodbye will set the fuse for a sexual bomb. He can imagine the fuse burning white hot as she drives away. He knows she will be on fire from the subverting of expectation and her body will become aflame in sensitivity. This is what it means to tease.

A woman is like another

It is common for men to curse themselves with disbelief or to believe the disbelief that others pour upon him. What does it mean to curse the self with disbelief or to accept another person's curse upon our reality? A curse only works if it is believed. And how many men say to themselves "I will never find another one like her" – Or how many men have heard their friends/family say "You will never find one like her" – These are like voodoo curses upon the success of our organism. The greatest lesson in life for a man is to not surrender to disbelief in self and not to surrender to others fears. People feel alone with their fear and so they share it. People romanticize life which causes them to catastrophize reality. These people want to believe that a woman was special because it reaffirms the feminine frame of authority that everyone is special snowflakes. But that is not the truth of reality. Most people are mediocre and can be replaced. That is why we use the words "average" and "mediocre" because they are literal truths to the masses that surround us. Most people do not want to consider themselves or their love ones as average and so they gaslight themselves into believing in the specialness of individual humanity. A woman does not want to consider that she is replicable or that she herself may be an "average woman." Men who worship women do not want their gods in their minds to be lowered to mediocrity and so they protect women as "Special beings" – This is why a man will be inundated with curses when he talks about women in generalities and when he replaces a woman in his life. Many will step forward to give advice wrapped in a curse of disbelief.

What is the truth? There are a few rare spirits out there but we will most times not witness them. People are people. The vast majority of women are mediocre by the very definition of the word. Women can be replaced in romance. And this hurts people to hear. That is why they will speak of "Irreplaceable specialness" and a man losing a "Good thing" – Do not curse the self with disbelief. Did you lose a woman? You can replace her. Was she a good woman? You will find a better one. Replace curses with blessings. It is a mind trick anyhow and better to lean towards optimistic belief than to fall into pessimistic disbelief. A man is an organism that is crawling from cradle to grave. And that is why he must protect his self-belief so that he does not wilt before his time. A lot of the "One and only" type people believe themselves romantics when in fact they are the biggest cursers of happiness than any other. To tell a man that he met his "One and only" is cursing him. Why? What if the woman cheated on him? Think about what this over romanticization of a single woman can do to a man's mind. If a man's "One and only" betrayed him, is not that overwhelming treachery that separates a man from his own sanity? This is how my own feminine frame shattered from the deepest of despairs. When a man's "One and only" turns out to be animalistic is a mind fuck. The romantic fairy tale turns to animal kingdom. Flowers and chocolates turn to ash and bones. The truth of sexual selection casts its obscene light over the darkness of our shared illusions. We hide in the dark because we fear the light. We fear seeing that our reality is common and that women are controlled by mating algorithms that transcends even the best intentions. Do not curse the self with over romanticization of women and do not accept others curses of their over romanticization of sexual selection. Did you lose? *You will win.* Whatever was lost can be regained. Do not surrender to the dark fears of loss. Believe in the success of regaining what was loss but not just regaining but getting more from life. Aim high in the future and do not be frozen by the past.

Leaving

room

enough

for

shadow

A woman is ensnared by doubt in herself and belief in a man. Women are attracted to masculine leaders and this means that women are attracted to men who have a stronger sense of self than them. And what does it mean to have a strong sense of self? It means to be able to validate the self instead of depending on external figures to validate us. Remember, women use each other as emotional regulators to reassure their sense of selves. What does it mean to leave room for doubt? It means to not ruin our sexual negotiations. In the Art of War there is a great quote "Never interrupt the enemy when they are making a mistake" – This is not just true in warfare but in business and romance. But the key thing to remember is that this an allowance for doubt. An anxious man on a date will fear silence because he is clumsily trying to avoid killing the chemistry with awkward silences. But what he does not realize is that letting a woman hang on the edge of her own words after she speaks will most times encourage her to fill in the empty space with her own voice. It is a small spike of doubt that causes women to keep talking after finishing a thought. But this only happens when a man has a strong unexpressive frame before a woman. This framed expression says in her head "And?" without saying a word. It makes a woman doubt herself that makes her fall into anxious talking which conditions her for qualification mode. Letting a woman trail off without showing reaction will fuel her doubt which will compel her to keep talking. This spikes arousal as the woman begins to tap dance for affection. And then after the woman has a few "False endings" to her conversation; the man can ease her doubt by reassuring her need for emotional regulation. See? Women use each other for emotional regulation but women can be conditioned for emotional regulation by a framed authority. This is a major reason that women after they become emotionally attached to a man will begin to imitate his philosophies and personal tastes. The framed figure becomes a reference point for solidifying the woman's doubt over her sense of self. And this is why "Dragging a woman" by ignoring her messages for a period of time spikes her interest. She begins to doubt herself which simultaneously increases her belief in the man's sense of self. Why? Think about how much self-belief is required in ignoring someone. Think about the level of self-belief that is required to not need or be affected by others approval. Abundance of self-belief. This is why the more feminized a man is the more he will kill the distance in order to reassure the woman of his affection. She messages him and he messages back because it is the truth of his intent but not the ultimate truth of how desire is built. That is why these unframed men fail and get punished in romance. They do not realize that doubt is love. A woman should doubt herself and she should rely on stabilizing that doubt with her man. He becomes a framed stone that is a rock to her uncertainty of self. His "Amused stone" face shows a little of his intent wrapped mainly in mystery. This is why women reward the strong silent types with sex and respect. It is the mystery of intent behind the man's presentation of self that creates the doubt necessary for a woman to feel like a submissive follower. See? This is why feminized men need to not feel that inciting doubt is cruel or abusive. It is kindling to the flames of passion. Doubt is a man's best tool in romance. But he must make sure that he is on the correct side of the equation. He should be inciting doubt and not becoming doubt filled by the woman. How? After inciting interest, always drag the woman longer than she drags you. Express less. Speak less. Engage her less. Reply less. This will create more shadows of doubt for the woman to think inside. These dark pools of doubt will allow her imagination to grow which allows her to fantasize about the man. It will not only inflate the man inside the woman's mind but inflate the truth of his power beyond actual reality. But expanding the shadows of doubt only works after a woman is engaged just like a fisherman only reels in after the fish is hooked. The woman must be hooked on the man for the doubt tricks to work on her. This is why the "Hard to read" framed guy who takes the woman on an adventure and then fades will spike her interest. Once a man understands the rules of romance he will know when to distance himself to spike the arousal. Just as greed is good in the bedroom, doubt is good for romance. Remember, "Absence makes the heart fonder" --

The

promise

of

spring

and

the

joy

in

life

    When a man is ignorant of sexual selection, he will harshly judge the burden of performance that is required of him by women. Sexual selection is indeed vastly more unfair to males than females. But the more a man understands sexual selection the less he blames the algorithm of desire in a woman's heart. Women just want have fun. FUN. Why? Because women are attracted to life and want to enjoy life beyond the burden of existence. And who is supposed to supply this fun for women? Men. It is the responsibility of men to be beyond the burden of existence and to reassure women that there is more joy in life than despair. A woman is overwhelmed by her own body and easily becomes reliant on weak willed indulgence that clouds the joy in her heart. What kind of man is a woman looking for? A man who comes into a room like fresh air off a mountain. A man who takes her by the hand and leads her on an adventure. *A masculine leader who ventures.* The fundamental reason for this is that a woman must be reassured in biological reproduction. She must be reassured in the beauty of life before being impregnated. Women are dependent on men to overcome themselves to such a degree that life seems easy enough for propagation. This is the core of why men use their sexual energy to build civilization and to invent conveniences for women's lives. The base of a man's creative passions is to make life easier for reproduction. A man who presents "fun" for a woman is a man who shows that he is not only brave enough to live life but enjoys life enough to bring more life into the world. See? Women love fun because women need help transcending their fear of life. This is one key reason that the feminist movement is focused on lowering birth rates in civilization. Women do not have framed men who display that they have transcended the fear of life from their youths. These infantilized men hold tight to childish entertainment because they fear the responsibility of growing up. And what men need to realize is that "Fun" is when a woman is having fun under an adventurous/responsible masculine frame. It is the difference between the excitement had with a stunt driver and a drunk driver. This is why a man who thinks he is fun because he is infantilized is in fact creating fear in women. These women see infantilized men as irresponsible in a harsh reality. A woman has fun when she is reassured by the man's frame that is protecting her from the dangers of surrounding excitement. During the spikes of excitement is when a woman will bond herself to the man's frame.

What a man must realize is the women want fun because women want to be reminded of the fun of existence. And they depend on a masculine leader to show them that despair can be conquered. They depend on the optimism of a leader. And a leader creates his own optimism in life. The times have always been bad and they will always feel bad. It is our perception of reality that is in our control and we can alter that perception to one of hope rather than despair. Women crave men who have a supreme spirit of abundance because abundance is a reassurance to the joy of life. A man who is anxious, pessimistic, infantile and afraid of venturing outside his home is only selling doubt in existence. He does not believe in life and yet he still has primal urges he wants to satisfy. He is too afraid to leave his home but he still wants to penetrate a woman with his seed. Do you see the madness in this? Women are sexually attracted to brave, fun and adventurous men because women want to encourage men to love life. A woman seeks the man on the mountain in sexual selection because she wants to encourage the rest of the men out from the caves of their fears. After a man reads The Wall Speaks, he will realize that "To be a man is to bear the responsibility of all things" To blame women is to blame reality. To blame women is to blame the design that is meant to improve us as a species. It is irresponsible, childish and ignorant to blame women in sexual selection. They continue in their common genetic patterns to guide our species with the hidden hand of sexual desire. Women want fun because they want to be reminded of the joys of bring life into the world. And not just "Live" by crawling like a beggar to the next day but to LIVE without fear and with a heart full of joy in being alive. And while it may be mediocre of women to say they love to travel; it is the mediocre code in their heart that betters us all. Do not just sit in stagnation with a woman, supply her with a stream of fun and lead her bravely on adventures. This will remind her to not be afraid of living and will increase her sexual arousal.

A

man's

seed

is

more

precious

than

a

woman's

egg

A man should not waste his seed outside a woman. When a man expends his seed alone does multiple things that this chapter will discuss. There are many men who believe porn/masturbation causes a man to have bad energy or that it somehow increases his nervous energy. This is true to a degree. When a man is expelling his seed alone to digital imagery is an act of surrender in sexual selection which cause him to hold that defeat in his subconscious. And a man who has replaced real world pleasure with virtual fantasy is not only acting in desperation but is acting pathetically to himself. Should a man play with his own erection? A man may stroke his cock to remind himself his own excited power but he should hold back expelling seed. The expulsion of seed when alone has a dramatic effect on the subconscious mind. It shows that a man does not prize his own seed and wastes it outside sexual selection. Expelled semen is the white flag of liquid to a man's self-created defeat.

Another reason a man should not expel his semen alone is that it kills his sexual energy. Energy is energy and a man who wastes his seed outside sexual selection is lowering his own sexual ambition. Too many men in our civilization are lazy in meeting women because they are overly satiated with their own self pleasure. A man should have sexual energy that fuels his erotic magnetism like a frisky beast. The sexual energy should propel him into sexual selection or redirected to masculine ambition.

Women innately prize their egg over men's seed. A woman sees most men as having inferior seed that is not worthy for her egg. When a man retains his semen is a man who prizes his own seed from waste. This retention sinks down into his subconscious mind and reaffirms his value of his own seed. It will project in his interactions with women who will pick up on this calm confidence of self-belief. If a man truly believes his seed is precious than a woman will share that same frame of thought. And a woman is looking for a man who holds more precious seed than her own egg. This is why women seek the most prized men among their hyper competitive female sexual competition. Women will fight over the rare seed that they all want to be impregnated with. "Rare seed" is an algorithm that makes them select a man among many. A man must prize his seed when alone and he must prize his seed with a woman. The seed is not wasted. Its release is rare and celebrated. A woman will join in this special event if a man has established that the seed itself is deemed special. Men who waste their seed by themselves are men who do not prize their seed and who zap their own sexual energy by easy release. Sexual selection is challenging and that is why releasing the seed should be from achievement not desperate surrender. Hold back the seed and grow in power. This will soak the subconscious in self-belief and will reverberate through a man's behaviorism. It will project through subtle actions when he is with a woman on a date. She will know that he prizes himself because his spirit will glow in holy discipline.

The psychology of ghosting

We build our psychology atop the biological constraints that exist below us. "As above, so below" We stand upon the base of our existence and create a psychology to conform to that reality. Why do women like mystery? It is because their sensitive genitals are hidden from their view. Excitement outside knowing. "The medium is the message" as Marshall McLuhan put it. It is a woman's body that most reveals her thoughts. Her psychology is formed by what exists below her. What does this have to do with "Ghosting"? – What does ghosting do to a woman's mind? It spikes two things that are essential to understanding a woman's sexuality. Indignation and mystery. We discussed mystery but why is "Indignation" a positive in romance? Let us think about the body of a woman. To think about psychology, we must look upon biology first. A woman's entire body is an erogenous zone because what most excites her is beyond her eyes. This creates an electric sexual charge that disperse across her body. Her entire body becomes like a lightning rod to a man's touch and her body is the medium to her erotic fantasy. But let us focus on *indignation*. A woman's sexual heat spikes when the barrier is crossed between a man's space by the boldness of him transcending that space for touch. She becomes aroused by the boldness of a grope to her breasts because it is a mixture of erotic touch mixed with indignation in that overstep of personal bounds. Do women just allow anyone to grope them in lust? No. Why? Because a woman's body is her own possession. When a woman is possessed by a man it creates a sexual charge BECAUSE OF THE BOLD OVERSTEP. The man creates the sexual heat in the woman by using her as an object of desire which fuels her indignation. Remember, a woman is a dual being and her sexual desires are duel in nature. Hot and cold. Yes and no. Women are indecisive and uncertain by nature because of this duality that starts in their bodies' hormone flux, swirling indecision and rises to a dual consciousness in their psychology. The indignation of a man taking a woman in sexual greed would horrify the woman if he was unattractive and would spike arousal if he was attractive. Women want to be dominated and used by framed men. Used like sexual objects. To be possessed by a stronger force. What does it mean to grope a woman's breast? She will become flushed in sexual indignation at that act of boldness. The more a man possesses a woman's body as his sexual toy, the more the woman will flush in heat from the indignation of overreach. Let us zoom into the female body and see why indignation creates sexual heat. Males are the penetrators of our species. We penetrate a woman into the most sensitive part of her body that is outside her gaze. We shove the cock into the flesh. Supreme ownership. Penetration creates indignation because it is male greed into the female body. We invade the space of women and we make ourselves at home. What does it mean to come into someone's home and to place our dirty boots on their coffee table? An act of rebellion and disrespect that shows we have more ownership than they do. The same with male to female in our species. We penetrate them which is a literal disrespect to their bodies. Grope, penetrate and fuck. See? This spikes indignation which creates sexual heat as we venture into the cave of their fantasies.

Let us zoom out to the psychology of indignation. Women play sexual selection on easy mode while men have to play on hard mode. This increases the ego of women who are the selectors in our sexual selection. A woman sexual rejects most men and has her pick among them. When a man lowers a woman's ego creates a feeling of indignation. "Who is this asshole?" a woman will think to herself. Look behind the curtain. *Grope, penetrate and fuck.* A man who raises his pride above a woman creates a feeling of indignation in her because of her already inflated ego in sexual selection. This is one reason that "Dragging" and "Ghosting" have positive effects on a woman in sexual selection. To drag a woman after she communicates is to leave her in a state of doubt. Doubt over what? Her value in relation to the man. But what is mixed with that doubt? Indignation over the man thinking he is better than the woman. A woman will split her thoughts between "Is he thinking about me? Does he like men? WHO THE FUCK DOES HE THINK HE IS TO IGNORE ME?" - These are the thoughts in a woman's mind when a man drags or ghosts her. And can happen within mere seconds of each other. When a man ghosts a woman what he is doing is inciting her sexual indignation by dragging her in mystery of his intent. Leaving a woman alone with her thoughts is positive in romance. Why? Because a woman is dual. She is both a man's prosecutor and defender in her mind. This is one reason that a man who argues with a woman in a relationship will make her focus on being the sole prosecutor against him. But a man who withdraws from the argument thereby leaving the woman in doubt thereby making the woman become the defender of him in his absence. This is why a man during an argument who withdraws affection/attention for a period of time will be approached by the woman who will initiate an apology. It is because a woman is a doubt filled creature who will be the first to doubt herself in comparison to others. But not if the man kills her doubt by being reactionary in argument which reaffirms a woman's "Prosecutor mindset" – To argue with a woman is to encourage her to fall into her natural state of externalizing blame away from herself with deflection/redirection tactics. This is why men who argue with women escalate the argument.

Going back to "Ghosting" –It leaves a woman in a doubt state that has her thinking about the man with indignation. As we discussed, indignation is erotic fuel that is based on biological reasoning. When a woman is left in a state of doubt, she will play both sides in her head which creates a love/hate dynamic. Love and hate are both emotions on the same spectrum. What spectrum? The emotional spectrum. And a woman who is playing both sides in her head is on an emotional rollercoaster. A woman's favorite/most hated state of existence. Remember, women are dual creatures. To place a woman on an emotioal rollercoaster is to remove her from her boring life and to get her a little fun. How is it fun? Women love drama and when a man supplies a little drama is a man who understands that a woman appreciates the entire emotional spectrum. She loves to hate a man and hates herself for loving him. To ghost a woman is to drag a woman over the emotional spectrum through mystery and doubt. The more she thinks about a man, the more she emotionally invests herself into the man. And what do we all defend the most? What we most emotionally invest ourselves in. We protect our egos by defending our emotional investments. This is why although ghosting a woman will incite negative emotions in her, she will ultimately flip to positive to save face. When the man drops in to reveal himself to a woman whom he has ghosted, she will be ready to qualify to him. She will mad but it will melt away by her own ego defense of her emotional investment. The man set himself up as superior from his emotional detachment which further attaches the woman under his frame. An ancient reminder in her ancestral memory of men leaving for long periods during hunt/war. A return of the man of her dreams of whom she has pined for in his absence. Anger turned to relief. Indignation turned to sexual heat.

Ego

takes

up

space

What men must understand about women is that they love confidence. Women themselves will admit that they crave confidence in men as an attractive attribute. But what is confidence? It is belief in self within an environment. And that requires competency. A woman looks for a man who is confident in his own reality. But not just this alone. Women love men with egos. Why? Think about how much ego is required to lead a group of people. To lead others requires us to doubt others. And to doubt others requires us to lift our self-belief above them. EGO. It is not good enough to be competent but we must have a condescension to our confidence. The king looks down over his kingdom. To be arrogant is to have not only supreme self-belief but to have greed in that belief. Why? Ego takes up space. Those with ego are battling for room. This is why two men with large egos either become best friends or worst enemies. They are competing for resource whether literal or abstract. The man with the largest ego will either be the buffoon in the room or the leader. He must overcome tremendous shit testing to overcome the conflict of his greed. This is a reason why women are attracted to egomaniacal men. Women want to be associated with successful greed. They want to share in the resources of those willing to take more than their equal share. But there is something deeper to this. Those who understand the innate greed of the human spirit are men who understand the rules of existence. Who do we remember in our human heritage? Is it the men who followed or who led? We remember the men who walked tall and proud. The men who thought themselves the world's gift. This is the truth within them whether they realized it or not. Sometimes these men would be aware of their great ego and hide it with false humility or maybe the internalize their gift with a Messiah complex. Either way they are remembered for the bold seizure of reality by believing more in themselves then the surrounding masses. Whether it was Christ, Napoleon, Charles Manson, Adolph Hitler, Jimi Hendrix or George Orwell; they all had supreme belief in their own spirit that drew others to them. We believe in those who believe in themselves. We set the frame of thought for others to think from. No one follows doubt. If being alive is a soft sigh then having a strong ego is a roar. A roar against the overwhelming and crushing doubt of existence. Think about men who did not believe in themselves before they died. They are gone. They will be forgotten. They wasted their opportunity to roar. Lungs that gave soft sighs with God's breath. What a waste. Are you seeing how we see ego driven humans? Do you see why a woman wants to be associated with arrogant men? A woman is a mojo leach and seeks to feed on the strongest energy. She wants to capture the roar of the human spirit and give birth to its imitation. She wants proud children who reflect their proud father. But let us go deeper. Women understand the power of manifest. They believe in the power of belief. And this means they see men who hold irrational belief in themselves as not fools but wise. Irrational belief in self is the most rational state to exist in. Who decides that a man should lead a movement? Who decides a man should lead anything in this world? It is the man himself that lifts himself up to the throne. It is the man himself who believes that he should be the one in power. It is the invisible hand of irrational belief that lifts us from the faceless crowd into the spotlight. And women want to share that warm glow with the proudest man. But let us dig deeper. Women base their sexual selection on a shared competition between each other. Female jealousy is what arouses them. And women look to the men who get the most heat from other men. Why? Because men give heat to each other when they are in competition for leadership/resource. The more heat a man gets the more others see him as a threat to those elements. But it is only sexually arousing when the man maintains his dignity among the heat like a leader. If a man is getting heat (Bullied) and he appears pathetic will be a turn off to women. If a man gets heat from other men and remains confident will solidify his sexual power over them. Women understand that power positions get the most heat when they are seen as a threat. And who gets the most heat among men? Men with large egos who project arrogance. These men draw to themselves tremendous amount of shit testing which projects out that they are a threat to the surrounding men. (This is provocative game which is further discussed towards end of book) A woman will not only see the threat expressed about an arrogant man but will play devil's advocate for him. This is why a man who tries to convince a woman that a man is a jerk, asshole or "No good" will only inflate her interest in him. She will see the sexual insecurity in the "Nice guy" and will play defender to the man with offensive ego.

We

rise

above

what

we

must

lead

    The most repellent element in a man when he is with a woman is his own nerves. A woman wants a leader and a nervous man cannot even lead himself. What does it mean to become nervous with a woman? It means that a man becomes self-conscious and doubts his internal power in comparison to her. This self-consciousness is like a white-hot spotlight on a stage before others that makes us forget ourselves. It is a loss of sense of self. To become nervous is a projection of anxiety of that loss of sense of self. This is why a man can give a brilliant speech alone before a mirror but bomb from nerves when presenting to a crowded room. It is not how we are alone that matters but how we perform before others that truly matters. A man must master himself and be able to perform while others are watching him. Why? Multiple reasons in romance. First, a man must rise about his self-consciousness in order to lead the consciousness of a woman. A woman will doubt a man who doubts himself. The less self-conscious a man is with a woman the more self-conscious she will become with him. This will frame her as the follower and will place her into a qualifying position. But another reason a man must overcome "Performance anxiety" which is what it means when a man shows his nervous energy on a date is that sex is a performance. A woman is judging a man on how well he performs while being observed by others because sex is an observable performance. It is one thing to be good at something when nobody is looking and another to show others that same talent. A man who can only perform alone is a man who is stuck in a place of masturbation. Another reason a man must become less self-conscious in his presentation of self is that a woman is a mojo feeder to his own energy. Women will become nervous with nervous men but then will be forced to rise above them in leadership which kills their innate arousal. But the core thing about a man flipping his self-conscious nervous energy to self-mastery is that to rule others we must rule ourselves. The key thing for a man who gets nervous with women is that he is forgetting his role. To assume leadership is to assume a noble duty which allows us to transcend momentary suffering. It is the assumption of fulfilling a role that allows a man to rise above his own self-consciousness. He begins to think less about himself and more about the role he is playing. When we change our perception, we change how our body is affected by that perception. Think about why a man gets nervous with women. He thinks more about himself than he does about leading them. That is the crux of his issue. He becomes a nervous boy because he is not rising up to be a leading man. The role itself shatters the frozen fear that restricts our consciousness. Lift the self away from the fear by climbing into the seat of the role. Once we sit in the seat of power, we begin to shift our perception to leading those under our gaze. Once a man believes in his own power of authority a woman will join him in that thought. We set the frame for others to think from and women are inherently conditioned to join strong male frames. Do not think about how to become confident, just **BE CONFIDENT**. And from stepping into that power position, watch as a woman will begin to doubt her own power which will embolden you. Get past the initial awkward fear and watch it flip to her side. Rise above the self-conscious mindset with a woman and watch as she reveals the self-conscious fears herself. Many men are genuinely afraid of women because they forget the role they need to fulfil. They forget that the one who is confident will become emboldened by the nerves of the other. They have bad chemistry with women because they do not create the good chemistry themselves. The situations are uncomfortable and awkward only because they are the ones who are not creating the comfort for the situation. See? To be a man is to bear the responsibility of all things.

Under

no

enchantment

but

our

own

A man is both his biggest supporter and opponent in his own reality. It is our disbelief in self that creates the most chaos in our lives. It is our blind faith in others power that most disempowers us. What fear should a man hold when he is going on a date with a woman? What is she to the glory of a man? Think. We cast the enchantment of our belief upon ourself and another person's curse only works if we first believe their power source. Step beyond the easy hypnotics into the hands of your own dreams. It is the blessing and curse of our own imaginations that carry us forward in life. Who cares what others think? What good is a curse from a jester when the world is full of them. To be free of self-conscious fear is to doubt in the power source of the many. They hold as much power as we think they do. And why would we give them power beyond ourselves? *We are under no enchantment but our own.* A man creates his own optimism and a man builds his own self-respect. That frame of thinking is a spell that we cast on others which draws others into that thought. We do not stand tall because we believe in the power of ourselves but we are attempting that belief with the action itself. And then once we are standing proud others themselves submit to that overwhelming will which further emboldens our power. What power? The power we ourselves created to navigate through reality with the most success. Many guys fail with women because they do not believe that they hold more power of authority than the women before them. This doubt makes them submit in anxious fear which dispels their women of sexual arousal. What gives a man the right to think himself in higher authority than a woman? HE HIMSELF gives him the power of authority. Men must stand up for their dignity and must withstand the winds of doubt until they pass over. We do not readily believe others doubt because we do not readily believe in the power of others authority. See? Act like a king and not only get treated like king but get handed the keys to the kingdom. And from what? From the very belief of placing the crown upon our own head. It is the belief in self that carries a man into a place of authority over others. It is his own enchantment that binds others to his will. It is his own enchantment that protects him from the curses of others. The more we believe in the power of self the less power we give others. And the amount of doubt this creates in others will further embolden the structure of that very frame of thought. Power accumulates power just as wealth accumulates wealth. People readily pour respect out to those who respect themselves. This is the key thing to think when going on dates with women. A man must walk into the date thinking himself leader and the woman as the follower. Once a man truly believes himself to be the leader then the woman herself will join him only because his own faith in self is strong. She may test him initially but the longer he withstands the tests the more reaffirmed his authority will become. His self-enchantment will bind her to him. A man is under no enchantment but his own and he needs to fear only that power source. Be free from the doubts that sink weak men into submission to the wills of others. These men only believe in the feminine frame of authority because they have never allowed themselves to think outside that frame of thought. They are being led like sheep only because they have yet to summon the shepherd's spirit. The guiding force that compels us to authority over others. Do not hold on to the anxious fear of doubt but hand it to the woman and become emboldened by her lack of faith in her own power. This is sexual selection and this is why women have submitted themselves to men ever since the beginning. It is the code that surrounds the beating heart within them. Women are designed to trust framed authority and a man who projects that frame will lure women into it. Whether they are aware is not important but rather how they follow that lead is all a man needs to concern himself with. **SET THE FRAME OF AUTHORITY WITHIN AND PROJECT THAT AUTHORITY OUTWARDS.** A man is under no enchantment but his own.

What frame means to romance

After a man realizes the importance of emotional distance in fueling emotional attachment, he will realize how uncomfortable this state is at first. To inspire doubt in others requires strong self-belief. To measure out emotional distance between ourselves and women requires emotional independence. This is what separates men from women and boys from men. And this is what separates leaders from followers. There is a common saying that goes "Whomever needs the other least in romance holds the most power" What does this mean? It means to be the reaching figure in a relationship is to surrender power. The rhythm of the dance of love is that a man takes a step forward and three steps back. And before a woman knows it, she has been conditioned to be chasing a man's affection. See? But what does it mean to be able to step back from emotional validation? It means to not need emotional reassurance enough for this distancing. This is why this feminized generation of men who have been groomed for mother/son relationships with women experience deep discomfort with this framework of polarity. Why? They are like boys who rely on their mothers for their own emotional regulation. They want to be seen, heard and reassured. It is a weakness that exists within them. And what specifically is the weakness? These men lack an independent sense of self. Leaders are more distant than followers because leaders have a greater sense of self. And this is why women reward emotionally distant men in sexual selection. It is the mystery that surrounds this supreme self-belief that intrigues these women. Remember, just as Eve was overwhelmed by her ego in desiring to know the mystery behind the power source of God, all women hold this same thought. They want to look behind the curtain of power and see where the source of the power leads. A man who can manage emotional distance is a man who projects mystery around his power source. And a woman's default nature is to seek out mystery using her feminine intuition. Solving mystery is fun for women. This is one reason they love murder mystery shows. Men often confuse what is fun and exciting to women. These confused men who want to be "Fun" think they must perform as jesters which kills the mystery that surrounds their power source. It is more fun for a woman to be with a mysterious man than for a woman to be with a jester. It is the use of feminine intuition in seeking out mystery that is fun for women. And what mystery? It is the mystery of a man's self-belief and the mystery of his intent. Those are the two key mysteries that a man should be protecting in the early stages of sexual selection.

How can a man manage his desire in wanting to give emotioal reassurance to a woman? He must strengthen his internal fortitude by reading my book The Wall Speaks and practice the discipline of masculine frame. The more a man trains himself to rely on his own emotional validation builds his own sense of self. Also, a man must realize the process itself. That emotional distance after exciting introduction is like blowing on the embers of love. Distance in romance is like oxygen to flame. And a woman will not chase affection unless a man makes her move towards him. There is a skill to knowing when to pull back and when to move forward. But the key is to make a woman slowly move herself closer and closer without realize how much ground she has lost. The more ground a woman loses in love the more she will justify her own behaviors towards the object of her affection. Why? She is protecting her own ego and the amount of her emotional investments. This is why a man will see the power dynamic shift drastically in his favor after a while with a woman as she spikes her attachment to him which further increases that investment. Wealth accumulates wealth. Most feminized men who are gaslit into not taking power dynamics seriously in sexual selection are being conditioned to chase the affection of their women which deflates their women's sexual arousal. Chaos. A man who lifts the crown on his own head through increasing his power is a man who knows the sexual delight of women. To place the crown on the woman's head is to become a jester in her court. And mad queens roll heads.

Power

flip

In the beginning stages of sexual selection, a woman has the power of choice. This power dynamic comes from the exclusivity of feminine sexual access compared with the sexual access of men. Most men are thirsty sexually and have sexual arousal for more women than the women to have for men. A woman sexually rejects most men because she views her egg as more precious than the surrounding seed. And she is not wrong. Women gatekeep sexual access because most men are too weak to propagate. This initial exclusivity allows a woman to have a spirit of abundance during this phase of selection. To play with "Free money" is to be willing to risk for high reward. A woman has this relaxed attitude which gives strong confidence in her chooser stage of sexual selection. The vast majority of men have a beggar's mindset in the early stages of selection. Women's inflated egos allow them to flake easily on men because they have more sexual opportunities. But the relaxed attitude itself is what reaffirms the power dynamic on the first few dates. The woman grows in authority and the man follows her lead in sexual desperation. And this template for female power is how many relationships are formed. A sexually desperate male permits himself to be disrespected as the emotionally detached woman exploits him for her specific provisioning needs. The woman placates the man with occasion sex as he falls into a powerless and disrespected position in not only the relationship but the family structure. A man who believes he has lots of sexual opportunities will eventually have those opportunities. The thought precedes the reality. It is the spirit of abundance that attracts what he most desires because his intent of that desire is hidden. And women will sniff around him with their feminine intuition in search of the mysterious power source. Why else would the man be overly confident unless there was a good reason? See? This is the projecting thought that happens around those who showcase supreme confidence. They started the surrounding chain reaction of thoughts by first summoning the thought. *We create the frame of thought for others to think within.* Whom enters who's game? This is why women will test a man with flakiness/low interest behavior to further increase demands. Most women will play these power games with not only the initial approach scenario but in the proceeding dates. And a man who chases a flake shows his desperation which further solidifies the feminine power that controls him. What do most men do when they are attracted to women who show little interest in them? They increase their attempts at engagement. And what do these women do? They increase their authority over these desperate men while keeping look out for men with a spirit of abundance. Why would a woman want to propagate with desperation? This is why a man should not reward flakiness/low interest. If a woman flakes or is showing low interest, move forward to another woman. To move on from the woman is to display abundance of opportunity which itself will arouse the woman's attention. We have a world of men who need to detach from the sexual selection process by avoiding the pits of exploitation that some women place at the very beginning. They are playing with "free money" and so they do not fear losing men from greedy tactics. And flakiness is greed of self. It is throwing fish back in the sea because the boat is full. A woman who acts disinterested after a successful approach is testing the man for more control. If a man has a positive approach and the woman is showing low interest, what should he do? He should show her even lower interest. A woman does not respect a chasing man. And a woman only becomes truly sexual aroused when she is in pursuit. This is why a man should never give more attention to a woman who is withdrawing her attention. Most men do not obey this simple rule because they cannot detach from their sexual desperation. Their beggar's spirit either sets them up for a slave position under a woman's frame of authority or they scare the women away with the desperate behavior. Do not chase what is running away. Do not give attention to what is withdrawing attention. Do not surrender masculine pride for the hope of sex. Be strong and be proud. Project a spirit of abundance in opportunity and opportunity will come knocking.

Moths

to

flame

A woman craves to look behind the curtain of a man. It is the true forbidden fruit of sexual selection. The mystery of a man's secret being to a woman. Like God to man. We must project a shadow of doubt over those we love. A woman follows not the man but the doubt in her own heart. It is the anxiety of love that keeps a woman invested in a man. Women chase affection to reassure themselves of the true intent of their men. What does it mean to exist in mystery and be emotionally detached enough to cast that doubt on others? It means to exist behind the curtain of self and to keep secrets. Most men would rather share their inner realities than to exist alone with them. Leadership is emotionally lonely and that is why most men shrug leadership for equal cooperation. They shrug the burden of leadership because they require emotional validation over their sense of identity. God exists alone to Himself because the farther up a power hierarchy the more alone a being becomes. The bottom of a power hierarchy is like a flat valley where everyone can see eye to eye and hold hands. And the power hierarchy is a pyramid design because the farther up it a man goes the less room for others there is around him. To be atop a mountain is to be alone. It is lonely at the top and that is why most do not ascend. It takes tremendous strength of emotion to lead others. It takes tremendous sense of self to keep secrets and to exist in shadow. And once a man understands that women do not follow him but rather his shadow is when he will understand that he is already alone. Once a man understands that the more he shares of himself the more a woman will seek the shadow of another man is when is will realize he how the game is played. Do not fear what you must become. Keep focused on individual power and celebrate the company of yourself. Remember that we cast doubt over women not to be cruel but because we understand feminine psychology. They are forever curious of mysterious power sources. They want to know not the mind of a man in the valley but the man atop the pyramid. It is the leader who validates himself who most intrigues a woman. She wants to see behind the curtain of power. It is the curtain itself that keeps a woman around, not what exists behind the curtain. It is the doubt that fuels the passion in her heart and not the revelation. A woman creates the romantic fantasy of her own making by being placed into doubt. In the past, a man would leave a woman to be alone with herself, to pine for him with her emotionally fueled imagination before returning to heightened attachment. Women are attached to the curtains that hide secrets. Do not fear the distance necessary for romance and do not fear placing a woman into doubt over affection. Make a woman think about you by displaying a lack of need of her. Incite her to chase affection by withdrawing that affection. Understand that women sexual crave leaders because they crave the mysterious power source that exists inside the leaders. They seek to be impregnated by the mysterious power just as Eve with the forbidden fruit of her desires. To know what it means to be God in knowing good and bad. And once a woman knows the mystery it becomes bitter in her mouth. And she will be cast from Eden because she has ruined the mystery for herself. The thrill is gone.

We

cannot

escape

the

game

To know the self is to know sexual selection. We either are in direct sexual competition or we redirect our sexual energy to other pursuits. But even in redirection of sexual selection is to be confined by that selection. To know how we exist inside sexual selection is to know self. That is why understanding both the burden and knowing how to transcend that burden is how we know life from beginning to end. There is no escape from sexual selection just as there is no escape from body until death. We must live within the ancient rules that flow through our veins. To understand women is to understand being a man. Once a man understands the great burden of framed leadership that is required of him, it is up to him to acclimate himself to that burden until it becomes as natural as breathing. Then he will see that understanding frame and sexual selection not only benefits him in romance but in friendships, warfare and business. *The entire system of things is based on sexual selection.* All things made by man is a reflection of his base design. Our forgotten generation are clueless about women which is spinning the world into chaos. This ignorance of the foundation is creating infantilized suffering. Men who are ignorant of frame are men who are exploited within their relationships and unknowingly encourage their own cuckoldry. These men spread chaos as they rake hot coals of ignorance onto their chest and spread the flames of chaos all around themselves. These men suffer in want of desire as they collapse their relationships. Men who are ignorant of their base design are men who are easily controlled from the lack of anchoring of their consciousness to reality. They are like trees unrooted from the earth and thrown about with the feminine winds of chaos. Once we know the game, we can win the game. And once men understand the common blueprints of women, they can begin to empower themselves over women. Women crave submission to masculine authority. The more women that are outside masculine authority the more chaos spreads in the world. We are seeing this more and more in our times. What happens to a woman outside strong masculine frame? Her neuroticism begins to increase and she is swept up in deadly utopian politics to solve all her sufferings. She becomes a walking vulgarity because she is in revolt against purity. Dyed hair, pierced skin and tattoos. She represents nihilistic pain and anxious suffering. And we are having more of these psychotic women beginning to rule our communities. They live in perpetual Disneyfied Sodom and Gomorrah. With one hand they hold the cartoons that cradles their cherished infantilization and with the other they hold non normative sex. A total absence of responsibility to their biological design. The mixture of cartoon and sex is their worldview. And we are seeing this spread out from these tormented women who hate human life while they attempt to indoctrinate the young into their cartoon sexual lifestyle. A man in dating will encounter these broken women who have severe psychotic issues. They will want the men to submit to them and join them in hating the male gender. The one thing they hate more than life itself is male authority. Not in truth as they will submit to frame with enough effort but in mock testing. These women are like wild stallions that require extra strength of frame to encourage submission. They are women like all women and crave submission under frame. But a man must be careful with these types as they are loaded down with emotional baggage that will end up making the relationship more challenging than it needs to be. But these women are not without hope. Men who adopt these women under their frame will see them become docile and content. Their neurotic self-harm will disappear as they find meaning in the natural rhythm of sexual selection. They have spent their lives swimming against the current and once men frame them they will relax into the natural flow. Years of self-hatred will flip to self-love as they grow to love their feminine selves. To be a woman is a glorious thing and a woman cannot be feminine alone. She requires the polarity of masculine frame to fall into her feminine frame. *The sexual chaos we see in modern times is all men's fault.* Men have abandoned their burden and so women war against men. It will be up to men to not only admit the burden of sexual selection but to transcend that burden to reassure women. We must acknowledge the basics of sexual selection and then transcend that burden. A house built on sand will sink into chaos just as a world that ignores that base reality of human existence will sink into nihilistic despair.

A

man

should

be

a

smooth

stone

    In The Wall Speaks I wrote about how a man who masters his facial expressions will be able to achieve an "Amused stone" presentation of self. This means to control expression to such as degree that a micro expression can be interpreted by a woman who is searching the face. It allows a woman to use her feminine intuition to unpack the man's thoughts through the subtly of his behavior. In this chapter I will discuss why a man should be a "Smooth stone" Many times a man will hear women talk about how a certain man is "smooth" This language is used with men who are players and who game women. These women do not hate these men but rather speak of them with a certain level of charm even if they themselves are gamed by the men. Why would women speak fondly of men who fool them? It comes from multiple reasons.

A woman wants to be bad without carrying the responsibility for the bad behaviors. This is why women like "Bad boys" because they can experience animal excitement while placing the animal behavior on the man himself. It frees them of accountability for the base pleasures. And how does a woman get to this point in her sexual selection? She is made a fool without feeling like a fool. How? It is the man who wins negotiations without making a woman feel like she is losing negotiations. A good negotiator makes both sides feel like they are winning even when he is taking the majority share. In the beginning of sexual selection, a woman will test a man's strength of negotiation. For example, a man may say "Lets meet Tuesday" and the woman will say "I'm busy Tuesday but free Wednesday" Is this the truth? Most likely not. It most likely is a shit test for control. Women who say men are obsessed with control are gaslighting men into submission. A woman is power mad and she hopes a man will come and make her want to submit. Another test could be about the location of the meet up. A man could pick a location and the woman will reply that the location needs to be closer to her. Does she truly care? Most times she does not but she is testing the waters of control up front. She wants to see how easy the man is to control by establishing demands. How does man overcome this? He must always ask for what he wants plus another half. This allows a woman to negotiate without the man losing ground. In the case of the man who picks Tuesday but the woman picks Wednesday; the man can say that he is busy on that day but would Sunday work? If the woman agrees then this flips back to the man's control. In the case of locational meet up, the man should pick a location that is a few blocks away from his home and if the woman asks for something closer to her; he should move slightly closer while making sure the location is till closer to him. See? Always ask in greed and then move back to a still winning position. This is the key to negotiations and this establishes a smoothness of control in the beginning of sexual selection. Women are built to test masculine authority. And thank God for that. If men were not tested by women they would not be sharpened for absolute power. A woman encourages a man to be strong by testing him in his authority. To be a smooth stone, a man must make a woman feel like she is winning even when she is losing ground. In sex, this could be a man asking for something sexually extreme to freak a woman out but then settling on something he truly desires. The woman will be relieved to agree to something that she would have initially argued about. See? Always ask in greed and then settle for truth of desire. Walk a woman five steps back and then retreat two steps. Keep repeating this until a woman is a mile back without realizing it. Smooth stone.

Another way a man is a smooth stone is by low reaction to shit testing. A woman will test to not just see if he is easy to control but she will also test a man to see how much disrespect he puts up with. When a man is able to stand up for his dignity without losing his cool is smooth stone. He must be immediate in standing up for his dignity but with calm charisma. A woman learns the dynamic of a relationship early on in the initial stages of sexual selection. She will either say "This guy makes my submission easy. I'm excited to be dominated by him" or she will say "This is a chump who puts up with disrespect and is easy to control. I'll exploit him for now until something better comes around" - This could be the exact same woman with the exact same man but is altered by the man's own behavior. This is frame. Weak men create cruel women. A man's own behavior incites the behavior in others. This is why a man should not take interactions with women overly personal. If a man works on his frame, he will notice the same women that would have disrespected him will fall into submission. A woman wants to be a fool without feeling like a fool. Women get sexually excited by losing negotiations in romance. They want fun and losing is fun to them. But only when they do not feel like losers. This is why they seek "Smooth" men to make them feel like winners even in loss. A woman will become bored and dry in pussy with a man she can control. This is the "Boring guy" - Many guys falsely think to be fun with women is to be adventurous or funny like a jester. That is not the truth of sexuality. Women get sexually excited (FUN) with men they cannot control and who sexually dominate them. To be fun with women is to be strong, independent and smooth in winning negotiations. The more negotiations a woman loses with a man the wetter she becomes. A woman was designed for sexual submission and that is why her body conditions itself for penetration by a dominant man. But since a woman has propagation fear, she must make sure that the seed of the man is worthy. For a woman to trust a man's seed, she must trust his authority over not only himself but her. The smooth stone means to win negotiations. The smooth stone means to be low in reaction to women's emotional testing. It means to be charismatic enough to make a woman forget that she is being dominated. This is the key to being fun with women and making them forget that they are losing the game.

A

woman

wants

to

narrate

the

story

of

romance

    Nothing kills romance more than a man who narrates the experience for a woman. Many men reveal their intent and hopes because they believe that open communication is what bonds a woman to a man. This is a lie. A woman is bonded to a man through her interpretation of the experience. Experienced men know to allow a woman to don a detective's cap in her use of feminine intuition. Women love figuring out mysteries and that is why women seek mysterious men. To kill mystery is to kill romance. And a man who hides his true intent fuels doubt which incites imagination. Remember, doubt is the kindling under the fire of passion within a woman's heart. When a man places a woman into a state of doubt heightens her interest. Why? Because she invests her emotional energy into the shadow of doubt and uses her imagination to realize her attachment from that dream state. The women of our species for millennia bonded themselves to their men by pining for them in their absence. For a woman, to be in doubt over affection is to be invested within that affection. And the expansion of the imagination is an ego fueled activity. A woman who figures out a mystery is painting the picture with her own signature. Only she truly knows and understands the man of mystery. Women are ego driven like this with their feminine intuition. It is an ego expansion pursuit that allows them a feeling of specialness in unpacking the doubt. What happens when a man robs a woman of her doubt? He reveals that he does not understand female nature and that he is a killer of imagination. Think about a man who tells a woman at the end of a first date "I enjoyed myself" Many men will say this to reassure the woman of their intent without realizing that they are robbing a woman of her doubt filled imagination. They are romance killers. This is something a man must remind himself in a relationship with a woman but especially in the beginning stages of romance since a woman is flightier before she secures herself with emotional attachment. And that attachment is formed by the mystery of the man's true intent. The key thing for a man to remember is to leave things undefined for the woman. How does a man feel about a woman? A mystery. Where is the relationship going? A mystery. Does the man love the woman? A mystery. The more undefined a man makes his true intent the more inflamed the woman will become in the doubt of his affection. She will daydream and daydream and daydream. *His mystery will impregnate her mind and give birth to her attachment.* The more a woman thinks about a man the more she will justify the time spent in thought. We all defend our own ego investments and a man of mystery will be defended by a woman who spends her time within his mystery. In my second book Our World of Illusion, I discuss the psychology of appeal of mystery on a woman in depth. *A mystery is to see enough of an object to be fooled.* Clues leading around the bend of a corner. Where do they lead? First with fantasy at the possibilities of realization. We first conjure what could possibly be before revealing what truly is. Place an object in shadow and we must conjure in our mind the rest of its hidden form. We must invest ourselves into the darkness of our own mind. This is the key to understanding romance and why many men kill romance by casting a hot spotlight on the bare truth of their lives and intent. An object of desire that is out of reach pulls us along. A woman who is covered in clothes that reveal her beautiful form incites our imagination through her modesty. Pornography is the stripping away of mystery for animal vulgarity laid bare. It desensitizes us to our own erotic imagination which our sexuality is based upon. Castration of fantasy by outpouring of the flesh. It is the same in bad writing. A bad writer will tell the reader what to feel instead of inciting the reader to feel. "The man felt sad over missing a woman" Or "The man looked out the window and remembered his first kiss. It had been over thirty years. The clouds in the sky were grey and no light was cast from them. The man stared up into the grey and imagined his love just beyond them. He closed his eyes and she was there by his side" --- We must incite the imagination to pull others towards us. This means we must learn to leave something to mystery and to leave things undefined. We must not bluntly force a narrative onto a woman but rather allow her to form her own narrative. "Is he thinking about me? Does he like me? Does he have feelings for me? What is he doing right now?" All these thoughts could spin around a woman's mind in just mere seconds. The more a man places himself in shadow the more inflated his image will become inside a woman's heart. Love is mystery. Love is doubt. Love is undefined. It takes great strength to not force our own narrative on others. Men reveal themselves from internal weakness. They reveal themselves like boys before mothers. They reveal themselves for instant feedback as a reassurance of their own emotional doubt. See? When a man is saying "I had a good time tonight" is a man wanting to not only reassure a woman of his intent but also seeking emotional reassurance from the woman. Always let the woman reveal her romantic feelings first in dating. A man should not say "I like you" but rather display himself through actions like initiating a kiss or calling a woman after a few days. This is how he says "I like you" without losing charisma. Let actions speak and hide the intent from the mouth. The more we leave undefined for women is what they consider "Fun" because it allows them to play detective which is the most fun for them. A major reason why women love true crime and murder entertainment. Playing detective is a pastime for them. Most men do not realize that women are in constant examination of them. A woman will notice every little scratch on a man's car, how clean he keeps his house and why he has an unopened package sitting on a counter. She will notice every little thing while the man is only concerning himself with her. Women are information sponges for men they are interested in. They will research as much about the man as possible in their free time. This detective behavior comes from being the weaker physical being which takes not only more forethought in protecting themselves but also in knowing the seed of a man has been verified by their sense of intuition. While a man can "Game" a woman in romance, romance is a "Game" to a woman just as much. The adventure in revealing the mystery behind a man is the heart of fun within a woman. But only if the man leaves mystery undefined for her.

There

are

two

roads

The first moment a man interacts with a woman in romance is an establishment or surrender of frame. And the woman will either dismiss a man's weak frame or will seize the opportunity for exploitation. This initial frame will either allow a man to take comfortable possession of a woman or will allow the woman to take comfortable exploitation of the man. The core of why a man allows a woman to dominate him is based on his own lack of belief in his authority and his willingness to sacrifice dignity for sex. This dynamic will increase the strength of frame of the woman from the man's weakness. He creates the cage of his own making that will eventually create chaos for his life. A woman will shit test the man's authority in the beginning to see which road they will go down. If the man fails shit tests, it will embolden the woman in her own sense of authority. One is always emboldened by the others weakness. The conflict for control between men and woman is as natural as the air we breathe. All living organisms are in constant conflict with each other for dominance. This is the natural way of things and romance is no different. A man must assume his own authority over the woman in the beginning of sexual selection. And then he most slowly begin to assume ownership over her. He must possess her mind to possess her body. A woman wants to be possessed and owned to feel that she belongs. Women are naturally social creatures because they crave a *sense of belonging*. To whom do they belong to? A woman dispossessed by a man's frame will fall into easy despair because freedom is tyranny to women. They hate individual liberty because they hate being outside the authority of men. When a woman is possessed by a man, she will offer herself up willingly for his pleasure. His pleasures become her pleasures. His identity becomes her identity. This is why we see identity crisis skyrocketing in our modern times. It is because we have record numbers of women outside the authority of men. They are lost, depressed and in despair. They belong to no one but themselves and this spirals them into madness. A woman craves belonging. When a man shrugs frame, his woman feels lost because she becomes dispossessed and this lack of belonging opens her up to infidelity.

In the beginning of sexual selection, it is crucial that a man sets the frame for his own authority over the woman. This takes time to make a woman crave to be possessed by the man. The man must assume ownership in small ways. A touch that goes beyond the touch of a regular interaction. Boldness in possession. See? We are not friends but something more. This is what a man thinks when he smiles with the woman before touching her leg softly. A conditioning for possession. When a man drags a woman in mystery after a date is a man taking possession of a woman's thoughts. She thinks about him and he possesses her. A woman is an empty vessel that craves to be filled by a man's strength of frame. The most common issue in romance for women is that they go on dates with men who do not take a strong lead and who show weakness when tested. The possession of power must be assumed from the first approach to the next date and throughout the entire relationship. A man's power over a woman must increase every day. She becomes less of herself and more a reflection of the man she is with. Her identity becomes his identity. This is possession. And what is love? A woman who is IN love with a man sacrifices her sense of self to the man she wants to be possessed by. Know the dance. Five steps forward and two steps back. Know the dance of love. Move her back through every interaction. She is entranced by the man's smooth power gains. Remember, women call men "Smooth" when they are fooled without being made to feel a fool. They celebrate their power loss because it is done with charisma. A woman holds tremendous pride and does not want to submit to weakness. And why should she? Our species would fail if women submitted their wombs to weak seed. They crave to submit to a man who makes submission fun for them. And this requires a man to make a woman feel excitement while she is sacrificing her dignity. How does a woman feel when she is around a man who assumes authority and projects seamless power over her? She becomes sexually aroused and this prepares her for penetration. This is FUN for woman. A woman wants to submit to the proudest man available. She wants to submit to a man who makes her feel excited in that submission. This requires a man to have tremendous self-belief in his authority and to be free from doubt over that authority. In a way, this is like a prince who is awaiting the crown. This prince will act with supreme authority which further emboldens him because he knows it is his right. The same for men over women. We see our authority as our right and this allows us to assume that role because the invisible crown rests upon our head. A woman will try to tip the crown off through tests but the man who maintains his composure will strengthen his woman's faith in his rule. Shit tests are opportunities to reaffirm authority when passed. Men who incite interest through the mystery of their power will engage women's interest. That interest will become emotional attachment the more women invest their thoughts and the more the men assume possession of the women's bodies. Mind and body. See? Will a woman allow just any man to touch her ass? No. But when a man confidently holds a woman's ass in his hands after establishing trust will increase his possession over her. Small possessions fuel greater possessions. Why? A woman is constant ego defense over what she allows to happen to her body. She will say "I would not just let any loser to touch my ass" It is a woman's ego defense that increase the power that a man holds over her. It is the initial boldness of a man towards a woman's body that fuels his possession over her mind. And vice versa. The more a man acts in greed over a woman's time/body the more the woman will justify the man in her mind. She acts as defendant not for the man but for herself in submitting to the man. The possession of the woman's mind begins with the introduction that allows her to daydream. And a woman would not waste time daydreaming about a loser. Or would she? See? A woman will flip back and forth between that thought as the initial stages of sexual selection begin. Then when a man goes on a date and assumes leadership over the woman in directing her through the experience; the woman will think "I would not just let any man lead me like he does" Is that true? Not necessarily. It is the behaviorism she is judging and not the man himself. It is the presentation of self she is judging and not the truth of fear in his heart. A touch on the hand. Possession. A kiss at the end of the date. Possession. Silence of a few days. Her mind is possessed. She is wanting to belong to him. She is wanting to be owned by him. He makes it easy and she wants to be easy for him. This is what it means to possess a woman. It is mind and body. It is body and mind. Each fuels the other as the woman justifies her own feelings that the man himself created. She justifies each bold physical escalation which solidifies the man's control over her. His dominance and her submission. And his power should expand every day that their relationship grows.

A

woman

just

wants

fun

Men will hear that "Women just want to have fun" And men each will interpret the meaning of what this fun means to women. What is "Fun" to a woman? Let us breakdown what women must crave. Attention and validation. Attention from whom? Validation from whom? They seek attention from power and validation from power. To be the center of attention and in nervous anticipation is fun for women. They want to be on the verge of anticipation of positive validation. To be placed in a state of doubt over validation from a power figure makes a woman nervous in anticipation. And anticipation of reward (Validation) is when dopamine is released in a woman's brain. Most men hold no real-world power. But they all can hold the power of themselves and that certainty of power can be manifest over their women. This is masculine frame. It is power projection and certainty of self. Remember, a woman is a doubt filled creature who seeks emotioal reassurance for that state. She is in the valley of shadow one second and on the hilltops of reassurance the next. An emotional rollercoaster. And rollercoasters are exciting just as a woman's emotional low/highs are exciting. A man who places a woman in shadow only to cast a spotlight of reassurance on her is a man who understands how to incite fun in a woman's heart. "But Jerr, this is emotional manipulation" Of course. And we must manipulate a musical instrument to create beautiful sounds. Too many men fall into Jester behavior or qualifying behavior with women because they are wanting to be "Fun" They are driven by fear and that fear corrupts what they try to preserve. These men try to be fun and end up becoming fools to their women. They worry about loyalty and that worry infects everything they do. What most men do not realize is feminine psychology and so they end up being exploited from their ignorance.

Let us breakdown "Fun" to a woman. A woman wants to steal the spotlight of attention from other women. A woman is a thief in her heart to the desires of other women. This is fun. And dependent on a woman's peers; her definition will be different. If a woman's friends are all at a party than she will want to have fun with them. And the most fun she will have, is by being the center of that party. If a woman's friends are traveling the world, then a woman will want to travel to more exotic locations and show off her photos to them to make them jealous. This is all fun. Making others jealous is fun for women. But not just anyone. It has to be her sexual competition. All women are different to a degree in this because each woman is fighting over a specific bone with her peers. It is the "Bone" that they are fighting over that most excites them. It could be thinness. It could be fancy clothes. It could be popularity. It could be all of them. And it is the triumph of outshining her peers that makes a woman most satisfied.

How can a man manage fun with a woman? He must understand what the object of competition is among his woman's friends and provide that for her. Or he can isolate her from her friends which alters the competition altogether. Then a woman only concerns herself with the man's source of validation. If a man is more of a lonesome type, then isolating the woman benefits them both the most. She becomes more dependent on his attention and validation. Her doubt over his affection will become her main concern and his reassurance becomes the joy in her heart. This is fun. And this is the "Nervous anticipation" that women receive around framed men. They become nervous in doubt which incites their emotions. Their nervous energy puts them into qualification mode which both gives them fun and conditions them for submission.

Listen closely. A man creates the game he wants to play. We do not play women's games we make them play our games. Have too much competition in pleasing a woman? Get stronger to please her or change the rules of the game. Getting stronger to please runs the risk of falling into qualifying to her. Changing the rules of the game is the best route. Eliminate competition and/or create new competition. If a woman's object of fun is beyond a man's grasp, then isolate her within your grasp. She will soon only think about the hand of her master. See? Why is a rollercoaster fun? It is from the safety of fear. The simulation of danger. This is the core to understanding how to please a woman. Fun is what we make it. It is exciting the nerves and reassuring the nerves. This is fun. A rush that leaves us exhausted from the experience. Sometimes fun can be so overwhelming that we hope for anything but fun. We crave boring stability. See? It is the same for women. Why do women stay with psychopathic guys? It is not just because these women are afraid to leave them but rather, they fear losing the excitement. It is the emotional rollercoaster that a woman fears getting off from. She wants the highs and the lows of her emotional experience. She wants all the strings on her violin strung by her man's fingers. She wants to be played and manipulated. She wants to be placed in shadow and then feel the warm glow of a spotlight. It is a dance to the music we ourselves play of human understanding that transcends most people's view of what is loving and cruel. It is human nature. It is female nature. Keep a woman guessing. Keep a woman in doubt. Reassure that doubt. Be the attention she most wants and the validation she most needs. But only if you truly care about her.

A

shadow

is

the

trap

to

ensnare

a

woman's

heart

    The biggest difference between a framed man and an unframed man is that the unframed man does not trust feminine intuition. A big complaint of women in regard to men is that men do not listen. What they mean to say is that "Men do not shut up" – This is a clue to how women attach themselves emotionally to men. An unframed man in a cornball fashion dispels his mystery with self-narration. This narration of the experience is what kills romance just as sex explained kills erotic joy and a joke explained deflates the humor. Not only does it dispel the mystery but it is an act of condescension to a woman's ability to put the puzzle together herself. A reason why "Mansplaining" is hated among women. All women are detectives in figuring out themselves and the men they are attracted to. This is a key reason that women love to spend their free time "Finding out who they are" (Identity obsession) They like to think about their identity because they like to narrate their own sense of self. A key reason that we have both identity obsession and identity crisis from hyper feminization. Men must realize that they become like onions who allow women to peel back the layers one by one. What arouses a man? When a woman peels off each layer of her clothes slow in a striptease, it sparks a man's erotic imagination. The same for women but with a man's sense of self. He projects power and the woman seeks the mystery behind the power. Men who know how to perpetually hold mystery are men who know how to keep women perpetually interested. But what a man must understand that while a man is projecting mystery, he must also be leading a woman. Leadership mixed with mystery. Women must be incited in interest to care enough to figure out the object of their interest. The object becomes like a jewel that shines before being pulled into shadow. Many men will think that merely being a boring stone in passivity is mysterious. They fail in leading conversation which flips authority to the woman in the interaction. Think about conversation like a dance. In power gain we step forward five steps and retreat two steps. But expression itself is power surrender. Expression is a transfer of power. Power does not need to qualify or seek validation. This is why in conversation a man should flip the dance. Two steps forward and five steps back. See? To lead a conversation is to incite interest in a topic by giving a take and then inciting the other to expand further upon the thought. But what most men do not realize in leading conversation is that after they take the "Two steps forward" they will impatiently take another "Two steps forward" because the woman has power of self to sit a few second in silence. For example, if a man takes "Two steps forward" and allows the woman to take "Two steps forward" – Equality. But a man who waits a few seconds without expression or with an air of expectation of wanting more will compel the woman to finish in nervous motivation to take the final few steps. See? When a woman has good chemistry with a man is because the man "Just gets it" – What does he get? He understands how to pull a woman out of her shell and how to place her into qualification mode. A man who takes five steps forward in conversation with a woman who takes only one step forward is losing attraction. This woman will think this man is bore. Why? Because women have fun talking about themselves, not listening to men. Also, a man who waits for the woman to take the first steps in conversation is passive which is a failure of leadership. Many guys overthink conversation topics. Ask her about her day, dreams and hopes. Give her a little about you and pull more out of her. Be interested in life and she will feed off that energy. Remember that silence must be earned through intimacy. Women dread silences in the beginning stages of sexual selection until there is physical comfort. It is a man's responsibility to keep the experience free from awkward silences. This is "Good chemistry" –

A man who reveals just enough of himself to spark interest without killing his mystery is learning to master attraction. Most guys are either over expressive or passive in leading conversation. It takes a fine balance of knowing the rhythms of charisma. And charisma is about making the other ego shine which reflects back to us. I've listened to over talkative people without saying a word and afterwards I'll hear them say to someone else "I like him" – All I did was be a listening ear to them and they became drawn to that. Same for women. A woman will think more about a man who knows how to listen than to a man who knows how to talk. The key is to get the woman to talk more in conversation without falling into interrogation mode by asking question upon question upon question.

Hidden

power

is

sweet

nectar

that

draws

the

birds

Women crave power more than men. It is the power that exists within a man that is what draws a woman towards him. Authority of self and environment. It is the dominant will of a man that satisfies a woman. Relationships where the woman has a stronger dominant will than the man always fall apart from that dysfunction. Weak men create dry women. It is the strength of individual will that a woman craves in a man. And how he achieves his individual will is of little interest. Life and love are all about negotiations. We are either winning or losing negotiations.

This causes most people anxiety to hear because most people lose negotiations more than they win them. And so they hide in a slave mentality which causes them to romanticize failure to shield the root of their fears. The biggest loser of negotiations will be the more romantic one. And sometimes it is good to be romantic as a form of ego detachment. But better for the woman to be the romantic one in a relationship and the man to be the pragmatist. The more a woman loses negotiations in romance the more she will be attracted to the man's dominance of will. It is a man's triumph of will that creates sexual satisfaction in a woman. Why? Because a woman is design to be penetrated and impregnated. To be penetrated she must submit in wet acceptance. The more dominant a man who is free of sexual anxiety (Certain of his will) in his sexual authority the more a woman becomes wet in her acceptance of him. Giver and receiver. It is the nature of our species. A knowledge that is becoming lost with gender fluid propaganda that is designed to make humans forget the fundamental fabric of their consciousness. And beyond penetration is impregnation. This is why a woman seeks a man with a dominant will that overcomes not only her will but others willpower in protection of her while she has child in womb. Order over chaos. Civilization over mother nature. Conquer over conquered. Not a surrender of will but the triumph of will. The key to a woman's heart is held by a man who does not doubt the power of his own authority. A man who assumes the world is his dominion before seizing it in his hands. Winner of negotiations upon negotiations, Smooth stone that make a loser feel like a winner. The possessor over the possessed. Owner over the owned. Master over helper. Dominant over submissive. The holder of confidence over the holder of doubt. Do you feel the masculine consciousness rising within you? Read this book and reread it again. Let weak men read books with tips and tactics while you realize the foundation of sexual polarity. Think about a blowjob. Men love blowjobs but many men are deprived of them. Why? Because they are bad negotiators and not respected by their women. How does a man go about getting a blowjob? He must assume that the woman should already being sucking his cock. Let's take a weak approach for example versus a strong approach and this will show the power of doubt within negotiation. A weak man will assume that the woman does not want to suck his cock and so he will hesitantly equalize the situation by going down on a woman in expectation of receiving. Many men go down on women not because they truly enjoy it (They protect their egos by saying they do) but rather because that is how they navigate receiving their own selfish pleasures. Another weak approach is to ask "Can you suck my cock?" - This weakness will embolden the woman to say "Not tonight" or "I do not do that kind of thing" - How many guys have heard something like this? But is the woman being truthful? Yes and no. A woman is a master at the art of hidden language and omission of truth. What a woman is saying when she says "I do not do that kind of thing" is most truthfully finished with "...with weak men" And why would she? See? Men who have weak will and do not trust their own belief in power will get less from life and love. What is a strong approach to getting a blowjob from a woman (Initially)? Pull out the cock and guide her down to her knees while not looking her in the eye. Look at the cock and to the side. Act slightly impatient. A woman will fall to her knees in submission because the man is not doubting his desires. The lack of engagement will increase her doubt and will prevent a negotiation in the moment. He leads her in silent consent for his selfish pleasure. His pleasure becomes her pleasure and she receives him in wet acceptance. This is all negotiations. Love is a negotiation. Unconditional love is for mommas. Romance is not a charity but an exchange of desires. And a man is most aroused by dominance while a woman is most aroused by submission. The natural order of things. But a woman will not submit to weakness. She will not readily lose negotiations. Where is the fun in that? And if that were true our species would have died out long ago because women would have been penetrated/impregnated by weak seed who could not secure a family line. The key thing for a man to realize in negotiation is frame. How do players in poker bluff their way to a win? They inspire doubt in others. How? By not revealing their weakness with expression. We set the frame of thought for others to think from. When a man believes himself to be God's gift then others will test him. And if he navigates their tests with calm charisma like water passing over a smooth stone then their beliefs will be solidified. What an inexperienced man must realize is that it is not about taking all up front but rather taking more and increasing that gain over time. How does a pool shark win more money? By allowing inexperienced players to win a few games before the larger bets are placed. This is the same in romance. We do not need to win every battle but we must win the most in battles. This is how we win. And "All is fair in love and war" --

To

solitary

hunters

Men by our nature are less social than women because we can manage our lives without collective help. A woman learns to network at a young age from anxiety of being isolated from the group that she relies on for her emotional validation. This fear of disapproving groups is shame based but it ultimately protects women who must rely on others when they become incapacitated with children in womb. A man can manage a life alone because a man must be able to manage a family under his frame. His strength of will must be great enough to provide not only for himself but for others. These are reasons why there are more loner men than women. But a lone wolf type guy will have some challenge in securing sexual selection. Why? Because a man who is popular in his social life will provide a woman with an environment where she will receive more attention and validation. This is why a man who learns to socialize will increase his access to women. But this does not mean that loner men are not able to secure sexual access. There are two types of loner men and a man can alter his presentation of self to be the more attractive of the two. There is a man who is a nerdy loser who wants friends but they do not want him. He is viewed as desperate and needy which repels not only other men in friendship but women in romance. Then there is the loner type guy who prefers his own company over the company of others and would rather play by his own rules than the rules of others. See? If the first guy changes his attitude about his predicament, he will become more attractive in his presentation of self. Instead of him wanting what he cannot attain, he changes to not wanting what others desire. A mystery. Why does he not desire what women most desire; attention and popularity? Mystery. And women are attracted to what they cannot understand. The secret behind a man's confidence in his own reality. The secret behind his power source. But there are other reasons why woman can be attracted to loner type guys. To be separate from group is to be an individual and to be an individual is to have a leader's mind. To be separate from the many is to be above the rules of the many. Bad boy. Loners are outsiders and outsiders exist above rule systems. What exists above is seen as authority and that authority is deemed attractive by women. This is a reason why women are fascinated by serial killers and criminals. These men obey rules of their own making and exist above the law. What is above is authority requires power within. This power is what draws women towards loners who give off bad boy energy. If a man is a lonesome type (such as myself), he should lean more towards the appearance of rebellion than the good guy's fastidious appearance of obeying rule structures. This does not mean that a man needs to be a criminal to give off a bad boy projection. In a way, I probably give off both energies to women at times because although my individualism is rebellious it is tempered by my intellectualism. How can a man lean towards bad boy? Be selfish and greedy in sex. The bedroom is a great environment to display that a man is more of a bad boy than a nerd. How can he do this? Be a dominant fucker. Make her love her own degradation for your pleasure. This is "Bad" and shows that a man is above a woman's authority by his dominant will in his sexual pleasure. Another way a man can give off bad boy energy is by being both disagreeable and distant. Think about a loner guy who is agreeable and needy. Weak. Why would a woman want that to impregnate her? What does it mean to be "Bad"? It means to be rebellious to existing rule structures. To be above the law and anti-establishment. And what is our current establishment? It is a politically correct feminist establishment. A man who is believes in male power will immediately be seen as a bad boy in comparison to feminist men who align their identities with women. What is seen in equality is disempowered in authority. What is equal with women will be dismissed by women since they seek power to propagate with. A man who views himself as more holy in pride and who seeks respect over affection will lean toward bad boy. Remember, what is perceived to be above is seen as authority. To lift the pride above the woman is to place the self in a frame of authority.

Another way a man can lean away from lonesome loser to loner bad boy is by breaking rules. This can be as simple as taking a woman in a place that is forbidden. It can be as simple as fucking a woman in a place where they should not be. See? To trespass beyond imaginary lines that hold others back is to be seen as above these lines. (Do not get shot by trespassing and try to stay safe. Remember we deal in illusions) Another reason women can find loner guys attractive is that to be a loner is to be anti-feminine. Women are social creatures and being anti-social is not womanly. But also it signifies something important that women seek in men, ability to validate the self. Remember there is a big difference between being a loner and being lonely. A man who is lonely will be seen not only as in need but desperate. Two major repellents in sexual selection. And a man who is a loner but not lonely will reassure the woman that he will not rely on her emotionally. The key element to be a leader over the many is to not rely on the many for validation of self. It is the individual spirit that pulls a collectivist woman towards a loner. Being a loner is a burden that most cannot bear. And a woman does not want to be burdened by a man. She wants a man who projects that he is beyond the burden of reality. She wants a conqueror, not the conquered. This is why a man who is less social than other men must learn to overcome his feelings of loneliness. He must exist above his own burden of reality to attract a woman towards it. He must become a "Man of mystery" and not a harmless open book. He must be dominant in will and not afraid of his own desires. Then women will find him more attractive and his solitary nature will be a turn on rather than turn off.

Men

must

be

leaders

For many generations young boys have been conditioned and encouraged as future leaders. But in our fatherless times we are seeing women being empowered over men. And these men without purpose fall into weak willed submission under the feminine frame of authority. Why have men been purposely disempowered? Because male empowerment leads to population growth. Encouraging men to be leaders increases the growth of industry. Order and growth. Women in power leads to disorder and decay. This has been done on purpose to deconstruct civilization and to lower birth rates. Mainly driven by population fears post World War 2 and climate hysteria. To empower women over men is to lower birth rates. Why? Because women only want to propagate with strong framed leaders. To make men weak is to inspire birth fear in women. And to leave women to their own self direction is to leave them to procrastinate their biological reproductive abilities to later in life when they are less able. It is mind control to depopulate the earth and to bring about a new world order from hyper feminization. Women by trait personality are more "OPEN" than men. This is a major reason why gender madness is spreading to collapse birth rates. And why borders are being opened to increase the welfare state from mass migrations for total government control. Things are becoming opened and dissolved. It is on purpose to not only collapse birth rates but to collapse industry that is "Burning up" mother nature. The biggest fears in feminine consciousness are over population and climate fear. To disempower men is to lower birth rates and to deconstruct the industrial revolution. Weak men create fearful women. And this fear is spreading around the earth. Hysteria is rising because women's innate anxiety of self is not being checked by rational frames over them. Nobody could have predicted that the sexual revolution and hyper feminization would lead to record numbers of virgin men in our world. These men have been left to rot in virtual fantasy while women crowd the few strong men available in harems. These entitled women who do not need skill for sexual access merely need to surrender themselves to the men they deem worthy while mocking virgin men as "incels" – Sexual selection in our times is falling apart in chaos because of hyper feminization. Men are retreating to fantasy because the have not been empowered to reality. This is why I write my books. To empower men over womankind. A return of masculine consciousness to earth once again. Men who read my books will begin to understand the game. And to know the game is to win the game. This forgotten generation of men are beginning to wake up to the power that was stripped from them. They are passing frame to each other. Orphans help orphans. We are going to reawaken masculinity together. We are going to bring back order to the chaos. Each man who understands the simplicity of women will be able to rise in power. This forgotten generation of men will rise in leadership. We will once again prepare men as leaders in our communities. Women crave leaders and to encourage men to be followers is to war against our sexual selection. It sets up families to fall apart. It sets up men to be cucked by women. Chaos is spreading from male disempowerment. The end is near but the masculinity reawakening in nearer. Helping men in sexual selection is the most crucial mission in our time. Use this book in finding a woman. Use this book with masculine responsibility. Encourage other men to read this book. Lift yourself in power and then lift up your brother in mankind. The days where we laugh about "Easy competition" among our ranks is over. To laugh about how competition is easy is to laugh that our ship of civilization is sinking. The future is masculine not just because we empower ourselves but because we empower others. Our pride is not just ours alone but it is shared among all mankind. Learn game. Pick up, carry and pass frame.

A

woman

wants

the

secret

power

Just like Eve in The Garden, women want the power that is beyond them. They want the power just out of their reach and they will be daydream about it being attained. What does it mean to be confident in self? It means to be certain of self. The body is like a ship we navigate with our sense of being. Women are attracted to confidence because they are riddled with internal doubt in self. They use each other for emotional reassurance while being in constant doubt over their sense of self. It is a man's strong sense of self that most attracts a woman to him. It is the secret power that moves his body. It is the hidden depth of control that draws a woman towards a man. It is the "Knowledge of good and bad" that a woman is most curious about. What makes a man confident? What makes a man certain over his reality? It is his strong sense of self. What makes a man nervous and what makes a man confess? Think. It is a man's doubt over his sense of self. How he aligns his own self with his surrounding environment. The forbidden tree in the center of The Garden. Does it bear fruit or has the branches nervously shaken them all the ground? Christ once said in Matthew 7:16 "You will know them by their fruits. Do men gather grapes from thornbushes or figs from thistles?" – *Fruit is symbolism for behavior.* What do women most complain about with men? "I wish he was a better listener" – We show, we do not tell. This is masculine frame. And this is the key to good leadership. A woman is reassured by a man's calm leadership not by his profession of being a calm leader. He shows a woman that he is confident, he does not tell a woman that he is confident. See? Lead by example. Lead through behavior and not by speech alone. A woman will shit test a man to test whether or not his power source is real. She tests like she is shaking a tree to see if the fruit falls into her hand, to see if the power falls within her hands. This is the key to understanding sexual dynamics. And a man who knows what to expect will know how to navigate those expectations. A confident man who displays a confident presentation of self through his behavior is showcasing the fruits of romantic desire. He shows a woman that he holds a power that is beyond her reach and beyond her knowing. He shows her that he is a knowing creature that exists above her in authority. And a woman reaches for that supreme knowing because she too wants to know how to be calm within her body. She wants the same internal power of a strong man. She will align herself in imitation with her framed leader because she wants to share his abundance of self-belief. The masculine is order and this order is what solidifies the belief within and the presentation of that belief for others to see. We measure out our time and affection to our women. What does it mean to be able to be alone without being lonely? This requires a strong sense of self. A power that draws those who want to know the secret behind the power source. It is a spirit of abundance that keeps a man from acts of desperation. This is how men maintain good sexual chemistry with women or how they ruin it. A man who deeply desires a certain woman will act in desperation which will reveal that his sense of self is in doubt. The more he reaches for her the farther she becomes. He pushes her away by his lack of power over his own behaviors. Instead of luring her to the forbidden fruit of her desire he is pummeling her with thrown fruit. We must not want what we most desire. We must hide our desires so that they may be fulfilled. It requires great self-control to not cry when we want to cry. It requires great self-control to not laugh when we want to laugh. And it requires great self-control to not act in desperation when we desperately want something. It takes a supreme sense of self to project a proper sexual magnetism. It is a discipline to be able to trust the needed distance required for romance. It is a discipline to let the women swim within the pool of her own doubt and not splash down with her. Keep the power source close. Keep it hidden. Keep the mystery alive. And she will sit under the forbidden tree of her passion without wanting to exit Eden.

Tall,

dark

and

handsome

Women commonly speak of being attracted to "Tall, dark and handsome" men. When I was young, I believed it to be a literal saying but now know it to be metaphorical. The two literals are tall and handsome. The metaphorical is "dark" which means mysterious. And what is the mystery? It is mystery of not only self but of the secret power source behind a man's confidence. Women know that a confident, mysterious and charismatic man can overcome his physical setbacks. A man may not be able to change his height but he can alter his mystery which has the biggest effect on how a woman perceives his height and handsomeness. Think. It is not the height but the level of power and command a man has over others that is most attractive to a woman. Men who are short can still command giants if their frame is strong enough. And the element of "Dark" or mystery not only distracts from a man's height but inflates his physical attractiveness to women. Women will begin to see a man as more handsome the more mystery he projects. This is why a man will see relatively unattractive men, maybe without money with more attractive women. The key element is the mysterious darkness that projects out from the man that pulls a woman towards him. A short and ugly man who projects mysterious power will seem taller and more handsome after a woman becomes intrigued. Each man can become "Tall, dark and handsome" by focusing on presentation of self and the projection of mystery. How can a man appear taller? The mystery is a like a dark shadow. And shadows can cast in longer length than the object itself. It is an illusion of power that draws the eye. And women will focus less on the bare reality of truth when their imaginations are engaged. To be mysterious is to be an illusion cast from our presentation of self. Each man has control over his "Darkness" which is the greatest element of the three. How can a man project mystery? Frame is like a wall that is before the revelation of light within. The stronger the frame the more it will block the truth of reality behind it. The projection of mystery is enhanced by the omission of expression. A man who engages a woman's interest will lead her by the shadow of her doubt. When a woman is thinking about a man who is secretive, she is investing her time in him. The more a woman invest her thoughts about a man the more inflated he will become in her imagination. His looks and height will inflate from sheer fantasy alone. This is why a woman will rank a man as more attractive after emotional investment while a man ranks a woman as equally attractive regardless of emotional investment. And women who invest their time in thinking about a man's mystery will justify their use of time by protecting their ego. The more a woman associates her inflated ego with the man of her desire the more raised in appearance he will become. This is why short and ugly men should not give up on the crucial element of mystery that makes a woman overlook the other two attributes. A man may not be able to grow in height but he can always heighten the length of his shadow. Become a powerful shadow caster and this will bind the woman in her thoughts to your image.

Good

Versus

Bad

There are two fundamental sexual strategies for men. They either attract with love or attract with hate. A man may wonder immediately upon reading that last sentence how a man can attract with hate. This comes from provocative game (or asshole game) which I will go into depth about in this chapter. But let us dig deeper into the fundamental differences between feminine consciousness and masculine consciousness. Women will tell a man to "Just be himself" for multiple reasons that benefit and reflect women. Let us break that down. How are women benefited by a man "Just being himself"? Think about romance like poker. To be the self is to surrender to self. It a return to the mind of a boy who has yet to understand power dynamics. A return to innocence and ignorance. Sweet over sour. What is sweet about a man "Just being himself"? It is a neurotic and open display of his personality. This messy behaviorism is what makes us have affection for others. We see their honest imperfections and this endears us to them like mother to child. See? It is a revelation of the ignorance of power and a silliness that makes us love rather than respect. When a man is "Just himself", he is showing his hand. He is dispelling the mystery of himself for judgment. And women need to judge men for procreation. A woman must be certain that a man is truly what he says he is to invest her body for child bearing. Think about the level of investment a woman must place in a man to become impregnated by him and become eventually dependent on his provider-ship/protection. When a man is revealing himself (Or his true personality) he allows the woman to make easy judgment on his potential. Now let us focus on how "Just be yourself" is a reflection of a woman's own sexual strategy. Women by in large do not have the great burden of sexual selection that men have. They are the sexual choosers. They are the ones who judge the approaches of men. Men are the ones who offer themselves up for initial sexual rejection. And that is the key phrase. Sexual rejection. A man must become a door-to-door salesman in sexual selection as the initiator in romance which allows the woman to be the consumer or judge. (Women also sell themselves in sexuality but not in the aggressive salesmanship aspect but rather in the display window aspect) When a woman tells a man to "Just be yourself" is like a consumer saying to a salesman "Just be honest" and also in ignorance "Do not learn sales approach tactics but rather follow my own tactics of display case" – The display case does not need to move but rather sit. It is a state of being instead of a state of overcoming. The door-to-door salesman must learn how to handle rejection over rejection while learning to manipulate through aggressive tactics. Any man who is a salesman understands that there is an art to selling something to a person who has little interest in the object in sales. A woman does not understand the hustle involved in sex because she is in a condescending position by nature in our sexual selection. She is the judge and chooser which makes her a fool when understanding what it means to be in the initial stages of sexual interactions. She does not understand what it means to be a man and invisible. To be a man is to be invisible before the majority of women and to learn techniques to overcome that state of neglect. The vast majority of men are sex starved and will give sexual attention to most women. This allows women to have an inflated sense of self when it comes to sex. They merely need to be instead over overcoming that state. To just be yourself is to just be a woman. But let us dig deeper behind the curtain of human behavior. We hear women say "Just be yourself" in sexual selection and "Born this way" in regards to non-normative sexuality. These both are one and the same. The state of being and not the state of overcoming. That we are born superstars and we only need to learn to shine our light. And that we do not need to change ourselves but rather reaffirm ourselves. The fundamental difference between the sexes in their philosophical outlook is that women believe in the born perfect view while men believe in the born imperfect and must overcome that state view. This is why most feminist propaganda is based on French philosophy encapsulated by Rousseau "Man born free but everywhere in chains" – Or rather that it is the external that corrupts us instead of internal. We see this philosophical outlook exploding in our times because feminine consciousness is overwhelming civilization. This ideology is being taught to young and impressionable women who are attracted to it like moths to a flame. It does not challenge their feminine frame but rather reaffirms them as innately correct in their oppressed thinking.

    Now let us focus on provocative game (Asshole game) or building attachment through hate. How does negative emotion turn to attachment? A man must understand how a woman is triggered into sexual heat. Arousal in a woman's body is aroused by indignation. To objectify a woman's body by groping is to make her feel indignation. This is the core of why women are attracted to indignation outside their body. Remember, psychology is built atop biology. Our minds are shaped and formed by the realities of our bodies. "The medium is the message" as Marshall McLuhan said. The feeling of indignation is deeply sexual to women and to feel indignant is to feel a mixture of arousal and annoyance at the unfairness of a situation. Women love to be sexual dominated (But by men they respect) and that is a power disparity that causes sexual heat from the indignation of the act.

Most men are invisible to women. And to provoke a woman is to become visible. To spike her emotions is to cause her to feel emotions. And a woman thinks about how she feels. When a man gets in a woman's mind through provocative behavior allows him to attach himself to her emotions. The biggest confusion among "Nice guys" is why women fall for jerks. It is because what goes up must come down. A man who practices frame will realize that emotional highs lead to emotional lows. Peaks and valleys. When a man practices frame, he stabilizes his lows by mitigating his peaks. Many men do not realize how close love and hate truly are. To be hated is to be thought about. And to think about something is to invest our energy in that something. Love and hate both reveal a man from his default invisible state. Both allow a woman to invest her energy in the man's image. The greatest challenge in a man's sexual selection is his state of sexual invisibility. Most women do not understand this as even average looking women can feel the sexually starved eyes of desperate men follow and validate them. But to be an average man is to be used to women's disinterest. It is up to a man to make himself known just as it is up to a door-to-door salesman to annoy his potential buyers. And how a man who makes himself known is either through love or hate. To provoke a woman by spiking her emotions in one direction. This "asshole game" works not just because it incites emotionalism but also because it deflates the over inflated ego of women in sexual selection. Remember, as judges and choosers they are in an elevated position. To make them doubt that elevation is how men flip the script. To make them feel that the seed is worth more than the egg.

I prefer to use provocative game because to be provocative does not mean to be cruel. It just means to challenge and to incite. The opposite of "Nice guy" game. The key to provocative game is to calmly and confidently challenge women without showing doubt or emotionalism. Whomever loses their cool or gets heated is the loser in this tactic. Whomever allows themselves to lose their cool is the one in the subservient position. To be above something is to be above the feeling of something. To love and to hate is be caught in the grasp of our emotions. This is why the aristocrats, elites and royalty of the world have a presentation of self that has the appearance of detachment.

A man who uses this style must not only make sure to keep his cool but also to occasionally subvert a woman's expectation based on her emotionally fueled feminine intuition. She will think "That jerk will do this or do that" She is consumed and obsessed with this provocateur's behavior. But when the man alters his behavior is how he throws off a woman's expectation which causes an irrational feeling to grow inside her. A womanly feeling. He made her feel like a silly woman and this causes her to enter his frame of authority.

A

woman

must

be

seen

The vast majority of men are invisible in sexual selection whereas the majority of women are visible. A woman must respect a man to want to carry his child in womb. The act of impregnating a woman is a sacrifice of not only body but of a woman's entire life. For a woman to submit to this body and life transformation; she must respect the seed that enters her egg. Women not only crave special seed to impregnate them but they want to be seen with a man who receives respect in his reality. If life is like a play that we act out than a relationship is a spotlight upon the stage where a man and woman stand together before the audience. And a woman does not want to stand by someone who will embarrass her. She wants a proud and masculine leader. When a woman is standing by a fool, she will want to step outside the spotlight and exit the stage. *Social embarrassment is the greatest fear in a woman's heart.* But just a woman's greatest fear is negative attention in public, her greatest joy is positive attention in public. Social validation is the heart that beats in each woman. A woman does not know what it means to be invisible in sexual selection like a man. To be ignored by the majority. Men must transcend the default state of invisibility and make themselves known. A woman simply needs to be whereas a man must overcome. The reason I am going into depth on this point is that once a man understands a woman's fear/joy, he will be able to manipulate a woman from shadow to spotlight. To place a woman in a spotlight with positive attention and to place a woman in shadow to deny her that attention. What does it mean to make a woman feel invisible? It will provoke her because it is a rarity. A supermodel that is ignored will become consumed about why a man is not treating her like the others. See? It is flipping the script. If a man thinks his seed is more precious than a woman's egg then she will join that frame of thought. If a man makes a woman feel invisible than he will become visible to her. She will focus on why this man is not giving her the attention that she is used to. It is a common thing for a woman to become attracted to the one guy who is ignoring her in a group. The reason is that this man is making her feel invisible which intrigues her feminine intuition. She wants to know why this man thinks himself better than her and why he would ignore her. In a lot of dating books there is something called "Negging" which means to deflate a woman's ego through playful insults. It is seed more precious than egg behavior and it lowers a woman's innate elevated ego in sexual selection. I do not recommend a man to be cruel to women in order to gain their interest but he could be playful in subtle teasing which has the same effect. The key thing for a man to realize is how to play a woman's desire/fear of external validation against her. A man who behaves as if he is overwhelmed by sexual attention and who ignores most women's beauty is a man who knows how to switch frames. We are either the desired or the desiring. Women love men who hide their sexual thirst until the sexual act is upon them. It is the mystery of a man's desire and intentions that triggers a woman's imagination. To hide sexual thirst is to make a woman feel invisible which makes us visible. Understand how to use this basic feminine psychology to your advantage. And remember to always pride yourself more than her.

The

bigger

threat

gets

more

arrows

There is no gain without pain. There is not treasure without bravery. The more a man sets himself apart from others the more pushback he will get in return. Many men walk around dejected with slumped shoulders because they fear the attention they will receive by walking around with pride. It is the pride they fear and so they surrender it before any challenge is had. What does it mean to lift the chin and to stick the chest out? When we carry ourselves with pride, it will be seen as a threat to others low opinion of themselves. The posture of slumped shoulders that round around the chest is a primitive stance to defend the organs from damage from attack. To stick the chest out and to pull the shoulders back to offer the organs forward without fear. It is this fearless state that draws attention of those who think the fearless state is not earned. It is this fearless state that makes others think of the fear that holds them back. To stick the chest and chin out is to be free from the restrictions of doubt. And this draws negative attention because most fall into the shadows of crowds because they fear the heat of the spotlight. It is the spotlight that holds the most power in sexual selection. Why? Because what stands out from the crowd, leads the crowd. It is the leader that holds power of the many that gets the most sexual access. See? What is required to lead a group? Frame control and strong sense of self. This is why those who seek leadership will be tested. This is why those who seek to stand out from the crowd will be tested. We must make sure our leaders can handle tests without losing their cool. To lose the cool is to doubt the self. When we let others rattle our cage then we show that we are imprisoned by doubt. This is why confident men will get more shit tests from women. But the more they pass the tests the more their authority is solidified to those witnessing it. This is a major reason that women shit test men. They are confidence testing because confidence must be tested to prove that the authority can be trusted. The reason I am mentioning this is because it lays the foundation for why provocative game works. Because if a man is not being tested then he is not seen as worthy of testing. Remember, women only shoot arrows at men who stand tall on the battlefield of love. Women only shoot arrows of passion at men that are visible. That is the key word. VISIBLE. And a man who makes himself known in an obnoxious and arrogant way will become visible for attack. Good right? Depends if the man is talented enough in deflecting the arrows back at the women. A man who is obnoxiously arrogant will pull arrows to himself but he can reuse these same arrows against his attackers. Then his authority over them will increase and they will fall into his frame of control. The basis for provocative game (Or jerk game) is to incite heat in others while displaying cool. These men rile the emotions of women while showing that they are above all attacks against them. It is the display of certainty of self. It is the display of a strong sense of self that does not change from others doubt that is the ultimate aphrodisiac to women. Just as arrows can be redirected back at the attackers so can hate be transmuted to love. A woman would never test a man that she sees as sexually invisible. Each attack is an investment that further pulls her into the man's frame. But the draw only works if the man stays above her tests. Once a man understands the rationale for shit testing, he will understand to emotionally disconnect from the process. The more he emotionally disconnects and focuses on his strategy the more success he will have in this provocative approach. Growing up I would see asshole type guys with attractive women and hear surrounding women complain about these men. They were venting their indignation over these men's sexual selection strategy. These surrounding women hated the game that was played upon them. They despised these men's arrogance while being consumed in thinking about them. Visibility is the most challenging aspect to sexual selection to men. To become visible is to be given an opportunity to pass or fail. It not just the visibility but in how a man deals with the heat of being seen. Because a man who makes himself visible to his opponents will be attacked. This is why most romanticize and fetishize the shadows and demonize the light. It is the darkness that holds them safe in its arms. It is the lack of opportunity that is both a curse and a blessing to their weakness. It is a rare man who likes being testing. But understanding the game allows a man to alter his perception.

A

tale

of

two

hunters

Two men who have effective if not equal persuasion tactics for game are Bill Clinton and Donald Trump. Both men can persuade women with different tactics for manipulation. They are supreme shamans of manipulating not just women but crowds of people. And their styles of manipulation are different. Just like two hunters, they both get the kill but in different styles. This chapter will break down the psychology of their manipulative effects on women.

Growing up, I was surrounded by dominant women who would gush about Bill Clinton's charisma. They would openly talk about his smooth manipulative ways. His nickname was "Slick Willy" and this name best represents his approach. How can a known womanizer get support from women for his method of game? It is because his hypnosis *does not elicit indignation*. It is like a cook who warms up the water slow under the frog to cook it. Or like an anaconda that slithers slow around its prey only to tighten its grip into a death embrace. He talks in con style of playing both sides to elicit separate emotions while drawing his audience in.

His energy is harmless which allows him to close the distance between his target and himself. While he is speaking about feel good points of emotional interest, he will be transcending the boundaries of physical touch. His soft raspy voice and feminine frame view of the world allows women to agree with him and drop their defenses. This is the key thing. His style is to whisper soft nothings into the ear of women while confidently surrounding them with his presence. And once their defenses are down, he will attack, attack, attack. "Hello there" He says from afar "Let me tell you a story, it is in your best interests as a woman. This reminds me... of wait you cannot hear me. Why don't you raise the gate of your kingdom so I can tell you more about this...?" His manner is to lower defense and lower defense until the woman feels it would be rude to refuse him. By the time the woman realizes what is happening she will feel that to stand up for herself would be a lie to her previous submissions. Women forget themselves with him. This is what makes him smooth. And why women do not blame him for his womanizing no more than we blame good salesman who master their craft. It is not the salesman's fault for the customer spending more money than they can afford. See? This is "Slick Willy's" style. His style is a soft drugging which leads to an ultimate boldness that women feel they cannot refuse. Another aspect of Clinton's behavior is his subtle sexual display that let's women know that he knows that his presentation is a nice façade to his inner bad boy. Ways he does this is through eye brow raises for emphasis on key words when speaking, licking and biting of his lips on occasion. These are all subtle clues for a woman to pick up on using her feminine intuition to understand that he is holding back. He knows, she knows that he knows. And she knows that he knows that she knows. It is the subtleness of Clinton's sexual presentation that creates a smooth sexual display that does not spike indignation while he closes the gap. When he is talking, he will speak while looking the target in the eye before drawing them away as he looks to the side to present contemplation. This allows a woman to look at his face and eyes without the pressure of his commanding gaze. Then when he returns his commanding gaze the woman will be hit like a deer in headlights.

Now let us focus on Donald Trump and why his style is effective and yet openly reviled by women. A man will notice that the vast majority of women detest Trump. Why? He plays asshole game. And wise men know that women hate to love assholes. Inexperienced men will think that women are not aroused by men they hate. This is foolishness. Women will spend their entire day talking about men that arouse them and drive them crazy. This is Trump's style of game. If Clinton's style is to slowly turn up the heat under a frog than Trump's style is to spike the heat only to cause the frog to leap to the cooking pot of his ultimate desire. This is not only Trump's way with women but the way his manipulates the media. He did this with gossip columns in New York City to build his brand. Allegedly, he himself would be the one to give juicy gossip to newspapers as a way to build his brand. His approach is that it is not about them thinking positive or negatively about him but rather that they are indeed thinking about him. And he innately knows that women just like the media cannot help focus on drama. Women love indignation in their psychology because the sex act itself is based on arousing indignation in a woman by dominating her body as owned object. To grope a woman is to make a woman indignant, flushed and aroused. Psychology is built atop biology. And Trump's style of game is to incite indignation which causes a woman to emotionally react to him which invests her emotions towards him. Hate and love are both strong emotion that can flip to one side or the other within moments. Many women hate men they love because their emotional investment spikes them. The opposite of love is not hate but rather disinterest. A woman that does not love a man will not hate him but rather will be completely devested of all feeling for him. He will not be in her thoughts. She will be completely emotionally disconnected from him.

Trump understands how women work, he knows how to play them a few steps ahead just as Clinton does but in a more provocative approach. While Clinton gets investment by each lowering of defenses, Trump gets investment by the raising of defenses. Think about it like this. A hunter makes loud noises on one side of an animal to drive the animal to the other side where he placed a trap. Clinton will bait the animal closer and closer until it is caught while Trump redirects the animal to a location of his choosing. In war, it could be an invading army leaking false strategy to make the defending kingdom focus their armies/defenses where they believe the invader will attack while the invader goes a different way. But it goes beyond that. Trump is not only redirecting but causing his target to emotionally unravel in a fluster which causes incompetence in defense. For example, Trump will use provocation to incite emotional reckless behavior which causes not only heated indignation but unraveling of strategy. This style of asshole game can be used to solidify control by creating irrational behaviors from the provoked target which shows the target's incompetence while displaying the frame control of the issuer. A man who uses asshole game will make a woman feel irrational (Which makes her feel like a woman) and fluster her into his frame. The use of indignation is an effective tactic that Trump uses not only on women but the media which is mainly controlled by women. The amount of hate Trump gets by feminists has more to do with his sexual selection style than his actual policies. "Trump Derangement Syndrome" is just "Asshole Game Anger" --- The key thing with this style is to incite, incite, incite and then to relieve the incitation. The occasional switch from provocateur to comforter flips the emotional spectrum from loathing to confusion which allows emotions fall to affection. When a bunch of female reporters are ramped up in what they think Trump will do based on his provocative style but then he goes against expectation causes indignation because their feminine intuition failed them which creates irrational feelings that ultimately settles into affection. Why? Because to defend their feminine intuition, they must give reason to their emotions. And the emotion does not stay on hate but slides to the closest thing to hate, love. It is all manipulations.

  The different between these styles is how they incite indignation in women. The provocative style is openly hated and yet secretly rewarded. Feminist and feminine men will openly mock this style because it was most practiced by boys in their formative years that tormented them in some way. The women will have secret sexual desires while the feminized men will just burn in indignation without the sexual release. A major reason that the feminized men in the mainstream media spent time going at Trump. It was payback against all the days of being made to feel less than around provocative romancers while they imitated the niceness of women. These men believed in the lie that women want nice guys. Their tactics of flowers, romances and poems soured within them as they watched the jerk walk away with the girl of their desires. This primed them to hate all men that use this tactic in romance which informs their political and philosophical outlook on reality. Most actions by humans are based on sexual selection. It is the root biology of our species that informs our psychology. These styles of game have been used from the beginning and they will used until the end.

Women

create

better

men

Sexual selection for men is incredibly challenging just like life is challenging. To suffer without meaning is to carry pain with no release. We must make sense of our suffering to get relief. And it is through understanding the cruelty in a woman's heart that allows us to have empathy for her. When we moralize our opponents, we give joy to both sides of the battlefield. We do not fear the battle but rather our own surrender. This is why a man should recognize the greed in a woman's heart as a jewel in his own hand. But not just his own hand but rather all mankind's hands. The code that compels women is the same code that empowers men. Women reward masculine and framed leaders because our species needs them. See? Do not hate the game but rather your ignorance of its design. Once we see the design we do not feel as much pain in bettering ourselves to fit with it. Why do women so commonly flake and sexually reject men? It is not just because they must secure prized seed and a prized protector/provider for that seed. That is only half the reason. The other half is that men are emotionally traumatized by this frequent conditioning. They are desensitized by the frequent flakiness and rejections. This conditions them into a low emotional state necessary for rational leadership. And the more they pursue women through the frequent failures the more depersonalized women become to them while the more detached they get from their emotions through the process. A man who gets his heart broken for the first time will be paralyzed in a void of pain. This trauma will callous his spirit as a gift. See? Each emotional trauma a man receives is a gift to further remove the ache of emotion from his body. It is crucial for a man to have low reaction to emotional pain to rise as a leader over women. This is why a man must realize that the process of emotional pain he receives with women flaking on him, sexually rejecting him and breaking his heart is a gift that allows him to depersonalize the experience of not only women but life itself. To think with rationale is to disassociate from emotion. What does it mean for a man to get flaked on and for him to think to himself "Female behavior... but still why did she do that to me?" without feeling hurt? What does it mean for a man to get sexually rejected by a woman and to think "What can I learn from this?" without letting it emotionally harm him? What does it mean for a man to think "She was unfaithful but it is what it is. What can I learn for next time?" - See? Each failure we get in sexual selection is conditioning for emotional detachment. The detachment necessary for increasing our rational minds. To look at reality with cold eyes like a tiger from the bush. The biggest issue of our time is men being stuck in a feminine frame of authority where they moralize emotion. Listen closely, emotion is unnecessary for moral decisioning. Being emotional does not make us more moral. Hot emotion is a way for women to cover up their cold decisions. They walk with cold rationale and then cover up their steps with emotional reasoning. A dual state. But men who are controlled by emotion are full of self-doubt and easily controlled by women. They do not want to be shamed or guilted and so they weakly obey those who prey upon their weak state. This is why a man should cherish when women flake, reject or break his heart as not just learning experiences but as a gift of emotional detachment. The more we are traumatized by experience the less we feel in experience. And this not only allows us the emotional detachment necessary for rational thought but something more precious. To those that do not desire will have all their desires fulfilled. What does this mean? It means that when we do not care is when we get what we most crave. It is the disassociation from the object of desire that places it in our hand. Why? Because a spirit of abundance attracts. Human beings love giving to those that need the least. The rich get richer because the masses make sure they do. A poor man would be shocked at how much free things are comped to the wealthy. The state of humans is to steal from the desperate and to redistribute it to those that show least desperation. This is basic human psychology. And the more a man is able to disconnect from the process of his desires in sexual selection the more he will be rewarded. This is why a man must not let the pains of sexual selection sink him into despair. Take each lesson and reconfigure with a cold approach. Hunting is a cold practice. And the colder we are in our approach to life the steadier our aim at what we desire will be.

The

greed

in

a

woman's

heart

A woman has a lot at stake in sexual selection. Not only must she sacrifice her body and life from the decision of which seed she chooses but she must surrender her ego in love. Women want the very best deal for themselves in sexual selection and they will feel little guilt in attaining that deal. No woman feels guilt over wanting the best deal she can get in love. Notice my use of language. Best deal in love. A woman is a dual being who talks one ways and walks another. She will profess that power dynamics should not matter in romance while seeking the most powerful man to associate with. The reason for this is split. A woman speaks in encouragement to herself and others on *how things are supposed to be and not how they truly are.* She first lies to herself before lying to others. This is why women have a more delusional state than men. It is because they sincerely believe in *manifesting reality through spoken intent.* This is why a man should be careful around a woman who professes her loyalty. An inexperienced man will think that if a woman says she is loyal than she must be loyal whereas an experienced man will know that a woman who professes her own loyalty is giving herself a pep talk rather than revealing the reality of herself. A woman will say "I am loyal" when she is truly saying "I want to be loyal to the right man and I am saying this to manifest that state" --- This is why a woman will say that obsession with power is nonromantic while seeking the embrace of power figures. She hates herself for how she is led along by her own chemistry. She speaks in hope while walking in opposition to her own speech. The more experience a man is with women the more he will understand that their speech is affirmations on what they want manifested and not truth in itself. But there is a deeper reason that women want men to shrug power dynamics while they pursue the power that is shrugged. Most men are seen as weak to women and they do not want these men to have power over them. They lead men astray with speech to protect themselves against the possibilities of being impregnated by weakness. What a man must realize about women is that they rarely think they are lying since they hold innate indecision over their beliefs. They hold duality within themselves which allows them to profess whatever they feel in the moment as truth. They tell men that love is not about power, negotiations and deals while they seek the very best deal for themselves. A man who understands this will not be led astray by feminine speech. Instead, he will hold power in his hands and watch as women circle him in thirst to what he carries. He will begin to understand that women carry more greed in their romantic decisions than the average man. He will begin to see that a woman will calculate all the cost benefits to being with a man in romance.

She will list out all the pros and cons of being associated with the man. Sound romantic? Of course it is not. But after a woman lists off all the benefits of being with a man, she will then allow herself to emotionally open up to attach herself to him. The hot emotionalism will wash away all memory of cold calculations. See? Women are dual creatures that behave one way while gaslighting themselves when the need arises. This allows a woman to not realize her own greed because she lets the floods of emotion cover over all trace of how the greed led her to the object of her desire. This happens in the initial stages of sexual selection with a woman and also when the sexual selection falls apart when her needs are not being met. For example, if a man becomes weak in a relationship for any reason, his woman's cold calculations will return which will allow her to open up herself to emotionalism for another man. She protects herself from guilt over this cold state by gaslighting herself as a victim who is falling for another. It is common for women to tell the men they cheated on that they "Lost themselves" which is truth. They found themselves far from home and emotionally wiped away the steps that their greed led them to. This is the core of irrational behavior. To not be able retrace the logistics of our state of being. A major reason that when women are telling a man that he needs to be "nice" and give women flowers; he should be reading books on power dynamics instead. And when a woman is telling a man that he is power obsessed by seeking authority in romance is a confession of self from the woman. No one on earth is obsessed with power more than a woman. Whether it was Eve reaching for the forbidden fruit that would make her EQUAL TO GOD or modern-day women who forsake submission to men. Women are obsessed with power whereas men are obsessed with sex. Men seek power to attain sex whereas women use sex to get with powerful men. It is how our species survives. Women reward successful men with sex and these men reward the women with their seed. It is the power that is transferred from one generation to the next and women are the drivers of this framework. If a woman rewarded the least powerful men with sex, then men would not seek power. The pyramid of power would never be built. Civilization would have never arisen from the primitive fields of grass huts. It is the sexual drive in a man that wants to capture the greed in a woman's heart. She leads him along on the path of her desires of power and rewards him when he achieves it.

In our times of fatherlessness with the unbounded sexual revolution, we have seen the acceleration between the disparity in sexual access between the sexes. We have women on one side that are being passed around by a few men as they cover their growing obese bodies in tattoos while their male peers have zero access to sex which compels them to surrender their consciousness to virtual pleasures. They are worlds apart and they are getting further apart every day. Modern woman sells her sexuality through digital means to sexually thirsty virgin males. A supreme impotence and mass exploitation of male suffering. This is why I write. This state of mankind has been brought to us through the psychological condition of men to surrender their power to women. In the past, we would prepare men as future leaders not only because having rational minds leading us forward into the future benefits us all but because preparing men as leaders helps them in sexual selection. This forgotten generation of men must empower themselves over this lost generation of women. These women will keep doubling down on absurdity and will become more irrational the further they get from masculine men. They will begin to worship the decline. They will begin to worship the fires that burn civilization. And then will it all falls apart they will blame men. This is how the future is unfolding and it will be up to this generation of men to seize power before we are led further down the path of destruction. Be strong my fellow orphans. Be proud. Read this book over and over. Learn the fundamentals and keep growing in pride. The future is framed.

Printed in Great Britain
by Amazon